D0435677

RIGHTING FEMINISM

RIGHTING FEMINISM

CONSERVATIVE WOMEN AND AMERICAN POLITICS

RONNEE SCHREIBER

OXFORD
UNIVERSITY PRESS

2008

OXFORD
UNIVERSITY PRESS

Oxford University Press, Inc., publishes works that further
Oxford University's objective of excellence
in research, scholarship, and education.

Oxford New York
Auckland Cape Town Dar es Salaam Hong Kong Karachi
Kuala Lumpur Madrid Melbourne Mexico City Nairobi
New Delhi Shanghai Taipei Toronto

With offices in
Argentina Austria Brazil Chile Czech Republic France Greece
Guatemala Hungary Italy Japan Poland Portugal Singapore
South Korea Switzerland Thailand Turkey Ukraine Vietnam

Copyright © 2008 by Oxford University Press, Inc.

Published by Oxford University Press, Inc.
198 Madison Avenue, New York, NY 10016

www.oup.com

Oxford is a registered trademark of Oxford University Press

All rights reserved. No part of this publication may be reproduced,
stored in a retrieval system, or transmitted, in any form or by any means,
electronic, mechanical, photocopying, recording, or otherwise,
without the prior permission of Oxford University Press.

Library of Congress Cataloging-in-Publication Data
Schreiber, Ronnee.
Righting feminism : conservative women and American politics / Ronnee Schreiber.
p. cm.
Includes bibliographical references and index.
ISBN 978-0-19-533181-3
1. Women in politics—United States. 2. Conservatism—United States.
3. Feminism—United States. I. Title.
HQ1236.5.U6S35 2008
320.52082'0973—dc22   2007045018

1 3 5 7 9 8 6 4 2

Printed in the United States of America
on acid-free paper

TO MY PARENTS,
LOUISE AND GEORGE SCHREIBER,
FOR THE MILK *AND* THE HONEY

CONTENTS

ACKNOWLEDGMENTS

MUCH OF THIS project happened in isolation: innumerable hours spent alone, analyzing data, writing, rewriting, staring at the computer. Such isolation, however, belies the importance of my interactions and relationships with others as I produced this book. First, I would like to thank the women who gave me their time, assistance, and trust—the staff and board members of CWA and IWF who allowed me to interview them. Their names are listed in appendix B. Without their interviews and other assistance, there would be no study. In this regard, I also offer special thanks to CWA's Darlene Nelson, who arranged so many of my interviews and took so many of my phone calls. For IWF, my thanks go to Ivy McClure Stewart, who never let me down. Linda Phillips did a great job in transcribing these interviews for me. I also extend my thanks to the library staff at the People for the American Way. They tolerated many days of my perusing their files and monopolizing their copying machines. For editorial support and vision, I thank Dave McBride and Angela Chnapko. Specifically, I appreciate Dave's eagerness and efforts to take on the project and Angela's careful and thorough editing. Her sharp insights have made this a much stronger book. Similarly, I thank the anonymous reviewers for their feedback and wisdom. For financial and administrative support, I thank the American Association of University Women Foundation, Center for American Women and Politics (especially Debbie Walsh), Rutgers University's Department of Political Science, and San Diego State University. This funding also helped me publish an article that contains portions of Chapter Three: "Playing 'Femball': Conservative Women's Organizations and

Political Representation in the United States," in *Right-Wing Women: From Conservatives to Extremists around the World*, edited by Paola Bacchetta and Margaret Power (New York: Routledge), 211–224.

A special thank you is in order to Rebecca Klatch for her intellectual inspiration and willingness to help me think through methodological aspects of this project. I am especially grateful that, in the midst of her extremely busy life, she guided me through the initial data gathering for this project. That was truly a gift.

Throughout the various incarnations of this project, I was ably supported by many wise friends and scholars, including Kathleen Casey, Susana Fried, and Karen Zivi. Cristina Beltran provided me with words of wisdom and, perhaps more important, still keeps me laughing out loud. The many cups of coffee and hours of conversation I shared with Carol Zaleta and Darlene Glovinsky sustained me as I finished this book. I also thank Latha Varadarajan and Jonathan Graubart for giving me perspective.

This list would be woefully incomplete without acknowledging my dear friend Deb Liebowitz. Aside from the editors and reviewers, she is the only person to have read every page of this book—many times over—while it was in production. She never failed me, and I am obligated to say in print—Deb, you were right.

This project would never have come to fruition without incredible support and feedback from Sue Carroll, Cyndi Daniels, Gerry Pomper, and Anne Costain. I am especially thankful to Sue and Cyndi, who continue to answer my countless requests for professional guidance.

While some may consider family life to be a hindrance to productivity and workplace progress, I believe that these experiences allow me to lead a balanced, healthy, and more fulfilling existence. My partner in life, John Evans, is not only an intellectual inspiration, but he is a great friend and truly a good person. His patience and good humor were essential to me throughout this process. And for infectious smiles, comforting hugs, and inevitable laughs, there is nothing better than spending time with my two daughters, Dani and Karina. It is especially gratifying to hear young girls proudly telling their friends that their mother is writing a book.

Finally, I dedicate this book to my parents, Louise and George Schreiber, for giving me amazing siblings, boundless love, and constant reminders of what is truly important in life. They are my wings.

RIGHTING FEMINISM

Advertisement

TAKE BACK the CAMPUS!
COMBAT the RADICAL
FEMINIST ASSAULT on TRUTH

- Have you been duped by factually challenged feminist professors?
- Have you had your fill of "*Ms.*information"?
- Are you tired of male bashing and victimology?

Campus feminism is a kind of cult: Students are inculcated with bizarre conspiracy theories about the "capitalist patriarchal hegemony." As early as freshman orientation, gender "scholars" begin dispensing false and reckless propaganda.

Join the **Independent Women's Forum (www.iwf.org)** in our efforts to restore reason, common sense, and sanity to the campus.

Should you encounter an item of "*Ms.*information" in one of your classes, in a textbook, or a women's center "fact" sheet, let us know. We will print it on our campus website, correct it with accurate information, and politely inform the source of the mistake.

Take back the campus
Take back your education

For sources and more information, check out the Independent Women's Forum's campus website:

SheThinks.org
1-800-224-6000

TAKE THIS TEST: Here is a list of the ten most outrageous feminist myths. If you believe two or more of these untruths, you may need deprogramming!

THE TEN MOST COMMON FEMINIST MYTHS:

1. MYTH: ONE IN FOUR WOMEN IN COLLEGE HAS BEEN THE VICTIM OF RAPE OR ATTEMPTED RAPE.
FACT: This mother of all factoids is based on a 1988 fallacious feminist study commissioned by *Ms.* magazine. The researcher, Mary Koss, hand-picked by Gloria Steinem herself, acknowledges that 73% of the young women she counted as rape victims were not aware they had been raped. And 43% of them were dating their "attacker" again.
Rape is a uniquely horrible crime. That is why we need sober and responsible research. Women will not be helped by hyperbole and hysteria. Truth is no enemy of compassion, and falsehood is no friend.

2. MYTH: WOMEN EARN 75 CENTS FOR EVERY DOLLAR A MAN EARNS.
FACT: The 75-cent figure is misleading. This statistic is a snapshot of all current full-time workers. It does not consider relevant factors like length of time in the workplace, education, occupation, and number of hours worked per week. (The experience gap is particularly large between older men and women in the workplace.) When economists do the proper controls, the so-called gender wage gap narrows to the point of vanishing.

3. MYTH: 30% OF EMERGENCY ROOM VISITS BY WOMEN EACH YEAR ARE THE RESULT OF INJURIES FROM DOMESTIC VIOLENCE.
FACT: This incendiary statistic is promoted by gender feminists whose primary goal seems to be to impugn men. Two government studies report that the nationwide figure is closer to 1%. While these studies may have missed some cases of domestic violence, the 30% figure is a wild exaggeration.

4. MYTH: THE PHRASE "RULE OF THUMB" ORIGINATED IN A MAN'S RIGHT TO BEAT HIS WIFE PROVIDED THE STICK WAS NO WIDER THAN HIS THUMB.
FACT: This is an urban legend that is taken seriously by activist law professors and harassment workshoppers. The *Oxford English Dictionary* has more than 20 citations for the phrase "rule of thumb" (the earliest from 1692), but not a single mention of beatings, sticks, or husbands and wives.

5. MYTH: WOMEN HAVE BEEN SHORTCHANGED IN MEDICAL RESEARCH.
FACT: The National Institutes of Health and drug companies routinely include women in clinical trials that test for effectiveness of medications. By 1979, over 90% of all NIH-funded trials included women. Beginning in 1985, when the NIH's National Cancer Institute began keeping track of specific cancer funding, it has annually spent more money on breast cancer than any other type of cancer. Currently, women represent over 60% of all subjects in NIH-funded clinical trials.

6. MYTH: GIRLS HAVE BEEN SHORTCHANGED IN OUR GENDER-BIASED SCHOOLS.
FACT: No fair-minded person can review the education data and conclude that girls are the have-nots in our schools. Boys are slightly ahead of girls in math and science; girls are dramatically ahead in reading and writing. (The writing skills of 17-year-old boys are at the same level as 14-year-old girls.) Girls get better grades, they have higher aspirations, and they go on to college in greater numbers.

7. MYTH: "OUR SCHOOLS ARE TRAINING GROUNDS FOR SEXUAL HARASSMENT...BOYS ARE RARELY PUNISHED, WHILE GIRLS ARE TAUGHT THAT IT IS THEIR ROLE TO TOLERATE THIS HUMILIATING CONDUCT."
FACT: "Hostile Hallways," is the best-known study of harassment in grades 8-11. It was commissioned by the American Association of University Women (AAUW) in 1993, and is a favorite of many harassment experts. But this survey revealed that girls are doing almost as much harassing as the boys. According to the study, "85% of girls and 76% of boys surveyed say they have experienced unwanted and unwelcome sexual behavior that interferes with their lives."

8. MYTH: GIRLS SUFFER A DRAMATIC LOSS OF SELF-ESTEEM DURING ADOLESCENCE.
FACT: This myth of the incredible shrinking girls was started by Carol Gilligan, professor of gender studies at the Harvard Graduate School of Education. Gilligan has always enjoyed a higher standing among feminist activists and journalists than among academic research psychologists.
Scholars who follow the protocols of social science do not accept the reality of an adolescent "crisis" of confidence and "loss of voice." In 1993, *American Psychologist* reported the new consensus among researchers in adolescent development. "It is now known that the majority of adolescents of both genders successfully negotiate this developmental period without any major psychological or emotional disorder [and] develop a positive sense of personal identity."

9. MYTH: GENDER IS A SOCIAL CONSTRUCTION.
FACT: While environment and socialization do play a significant role in human life, a growing body of research in neuroscience, endocrinology, and psychology over the past 40 years suggests there is a biological basis for many sex differences in aptitudes and preferences. In general, males have better spatial reasoning skills, females better verbal skills. Males are greater risk takers, females are more nurturing.
Of course, this does not mean that women should be prevented from pursuing their goals in any field they choose; what it does suggest is that we should not expect or demand parity in all fields. More women than men will continue to want to stay at home with small children and pursue careers in fields like early childhood education or psychology; men will continue to be over-represented in fields like helicopter mechanics and hydraulic engineering.
Warning: Most gender scholars in our universities have degrees in English or comparative literature—not biology or neuroscience. These self-appointed experts on sexuality are scientifically illiterate. They substitute dogma and propaganda for reasoned scholarship.

10. MYTH: WOMEN'S STUDIES DEPARTMENTS EMPOWERED WOMEN AND GAVE THEM A VOICE IN THE ACADEMY.
FACT: Women's Studies empowered a small group of like-minded careerists. They have created an old-girl network that is far more elitist, narrow, and closed than any of the old-boy networks they rail against. Vast numbers of moderate or dissident women scholars have been marginalized, excluded, and silenced.

Chapter 1

INTRODUCTION

IN APRIL 2001, the Independent Women's Forum (IWF) ran a full-page ad in several campus newspapers,[1] urging students to "Take Back the Campus"[2] from "factually challenged" feminist professors seeking to indoctrinate students into a "cult." In the ad, IWF asserted that feminists had exaggerated the frequency and severity of incidences of violence against women[3] and that feminist accounts of gender differences in wages and gender biases in schools were overstated and often inaccurate. Finally, the ad encouraged students who encountered such accounts of "Ms/information" to report them to IWF for posting on its Web site. IWF caused a stir on several campuses with the publication, garnering the organization national publicity.[4] This was, no doubt, part of the intent of this media-savvy organization.

Upon first glancing at the ad, one is compelled to ask: why would a women's organization run this? Why would a women's organization publicly contest women's claims of abuse and violence? How can it square its need to appeal to women with its seeming disregard for feminist construction of women's interests? Can we just dismiss this organization as being antiwomen or the dupe of conservative men? Simply put, no. As a conservative women's organization, IWF was articulating alternative bases for understanding women's political interests. And it had clout because women were making the claims.

IWF's agenda in this incident is representative of a significant political battle that has been largely unrecognized by political analysts.

As women's political power has increased, so too has a contest among national organizations fighting to represent women's interests in the policymaking process. Although feminists have long dominated the political landscape in terms of numbers and visibility, they are increasingly being challenged by other national organizations—those that are antifeminist and also claim to represent women's interests. These conservative women's groups present a substantial threat to the feminist movement. They are well organized, politically active, and have access to government institutions, political parties, and national media. As these organizations vie with feminists over what women need and desire, they publicly contest definitions of women's interests and influence political debates and policy outcomes. Inattention to comparably sized and situated feminist organizations, such as the National Organization for Women (NOW), would be untenable; yet almost no scholarship exists on national conservative women's organizations.[5] An examination of these national political actors is long overdue.

This book examines the two most visible and prominent conservative women's organizations: Concerned Women for America (CWA) and Independent Women's Forum (IWF). CWA is one of the largest grassroots women's organizations in the country and participates in a host of current political debates. Founded in 1979 to oppose the Equal Rights Amendment, this multi-issue interest group rivals in size and scope its feminist counterpart, NOW. IWF emerged in 1992 through the efforts of women formerly organized to support the nomination of Clarence Thomas to the U.S. Supreme Court. Energized by their work to promote Thomas's appointment, these professional women dedicated themselves to establishing a national and institutional voice for economically conservative women. Featured in a *Washington Post* story that highlighted the organization's keen ability to get its leaders on the public airwaves, IWF includes associates who have positions in and strong ties to George W. Bush's administration.[6] Among these are founding board member Lynne Cheney, who is the nation's Second Lady, and national advisory board member Elaine Chao, who is the U.S. labor secretary. Given the growing stature of these organizations, it is important to understand their role in American politics. As policymakers take them seriously, both groups work pointedly to undermine feminist policy successes. And, because they are women challenging other women's political views, the media are eager to give them access; controversy generates interest and viewership.[7]

This book highlights the unique position of CWA and IWF as both conservative and women's organizations and explores how this status affects their actions. As conservative and women's organizations, CWA and IWF must behave differently from their male counterparts. Since they claim to be speaking as and for women, they not only aim to mobilize people around conservative politics, but seek to specifically rally women to stand with them. To this end, they organize meetings on college campuses, sponsor prayer groups, train lobbyists, and hold conferences, brown bag lunches, and seminars. Almost always, women are the explicit invitees to these events. In addition, both organizations take as a central goal the promotion of political issues from conservative women's points of view. However, they must also take into account the success of feminism in defining women's policy priorities and agendas. Keeping in mind this political context, questions central to the book are: how do CWA and IWF establish themselves as legitimate representatives of women's interests? How do being conservative and being women's organizations influence the tactics they choose? How do their actions shape the conservative movement and bear upon feminist activism?

Exploration of these questions also brings to light information about how specific conservative ideologies figure into action and underscores organizational distinctions among conservative women's groups. Although both groups formed as women's organizations to challenge feminist activism, they have different constituencies. CWA is a socially conservative interest group, mostly composed of evangelical Protestant women. It is concerned with public and private morality, opposes abortion and civil rights for homosexuals, and advocates prayer in schools. CWA also coalesces with other Christian Right groups that have commanded the attention of politicians and analysts alike. IWF, however, more closely matches the description of an economic conservative group, with its call for individuals' self-sufficiency, limited federal social programs and business regulations, and increased private sector involvement in the provision of public goods and services. With its libertarian leanings, it stays out of debates over issues like abortion. These contrasting positions illuminate the relative influence of CWA and IWF's divergent ideologies. However, there are moments when CWA and IWF express comparable beliefs and goals and behave in similar ways; therefore, examination of these two distinct organizations highlights the fluidity of the ideological boundaries between social and economic conservatives.

As other scholars have demonstrated, attention to context matters when trying to understand women's quest for "political standing" or legitimacy.[8] Being both conservative and women's organizations, CWA and IWF exist in a milieu rife with competing values and audiences: feminist activists, the conservative groups with which they coalesce, their members and potential adherents. Each group must speak to its own conservative constituencies and allies, but also appeal to a broader range of women, many of whom have benefited from and support the goals of the feminist movement.

But conservative organizations and activists have either been unsympathetic to many women's issues or have not traditionally taken the helm on the ones central to CWA's and IWF's agendas.[9] And, when conservatives have taken on policies that are of special interest to women, they have often done so in ways that alienate women who may otherwise feel partial to conservative causes. For example, there are many prochoice Republican women who struggle with its party's anti-abortion platform. Given this conflict, CWA and IWF must grapple with crafting messages about women's issues that ring true with conservatives and are potentially compelling to a broader range of women. In this way, they are always present as both women's and conservative organizations and reference themselves in terms that incorporate both of these identities.

CWA and IWF not only connect their members and associates to other conservative causes and organizations, but also strive to attract and mobilize women not affiliated with their organizations. Given that feminists have had decades to stake their claims to women's interests and have had a significant impact on women's lives, these advocates must take women's attitudes and feminism's influence into account. Notwithstanding political losses since the 1970s, feminists have greatly transformed the social, economic, and political landscape for women by helping to increase the number of women in public office,[10] changing beliefs about gender roles, and pushing for legislation aimed at improving women's lives. For example, in both the legislative and judicial arenas, feminist accomplishments include *Roe v. Wade*, which legalized abortion in 1973; the passage of Title IX, which promotes equity for women and girls in federally funded institutions; implementation of the Family and Medical Leave Act of 1993, which guarantees unpaid family leave to new parents and caregivers; and the procurement of significant federal funding for women's health issues, especially breast cancer.[11] CWA and IWF oppose a number of these specific policy achievements, but must acknowledge on some level that many women feel that they have benefited from these efforts.[12] These ardent opponents of feminism are compelled to make sense of their opponents' accomplishments, while simultaneously discrediting them as representatives of women's interests. If they fail to carry out this task, they will lose the ability to reach out to women who do not identify with any women's organization, but who want policy solutions that address the stresses in their lives. Moreover, the organizations must demonstrate why their perspectives differ from and are more credible than those of feminists. This tension must be accounted for when trying to understand the strategies that CWA and IWF employ as they strive to be taken seriously as groups that represent women's interests.

A DEFINITIONAL NOTE ABOUT FEMINISM

Feminists are not monolithic in their political views or organizational forms, but CWA and IWF characterize them as such. It is not just the tenets of feminism that concern them, but organized feminism's presence in political institutions, educational institutions, and the media as well. To be clear, when CWA and IWF talk about the feminist movement, they are mostly referring to nationally organized interest groups, especially NOW, National Abortion and Reproductive Rights Action League (NARAL), Planned Parenthood Federation of American (PPFA), American Association of University Women (AAUW), and Feminist Majority Foundation (FMF). In some cases, the organizations also directly and indirectly reference the efforts of individual feminist activists, leaders, and scholars. This is evident, for example, when CWA incorporates the work of antipornography feminists Catharine MacKinnon and Andrea Dworkin into CWA discussions about pornography (see chapter 4). The feminist movement in the United States includes other national organizations, community groups, direct service providers, campus-based groups, Web sites, and leaders;[13] however, CWA and IWF specifically name a limited number of feminist interest groups and leaders as proxies for the entire movement. To be consistent with CWA and IWF, when I reference the "feminist movement" or "feminists," I, too, am referring to these relatively institutionalized political actors unless I state otherwise. By way of definition, these feminist actors support women's equal rights under the law and believe that women's oppression relative to men is the result of discrimination. In addition, feminists believe that women's status is predominantly shaped by processes of institutional and structural inequality, not by individual actions or circumstances.[14]

CENTRAL THEMES: REPRESENTATION, IDENTITY, AND ISSUE FRAMING

To address questions about how CWA and IWF act to legitimate themselves as representatives of women's interests, this book is divided into two thematic parts. The first section, notably chapter 3, examines the organizations' "representational" strategies. Deliberations about the role of elected officials typically take representation into account,[15] but interest groups also represent constituents in the policymaking process. Questions of legitimacy and identity are central to debates about representation: who can rightfully speak for whom, and who should be taken seriously as a delegate for someone else?[16] Interest group scholars have narrowly raised the question of representation in debates over pluralism, bias, and the extent to which interest groups adequately and fairly typify the range of interests among a country's citizenship.[17]

For CWA and IWF, questions of representation are indeed salient, but must be viewed in light of their status as identity-based organizations. CWA and IWF oppose not only the policy goals of feminist organizations, but the right of those groups to speak for women. They are concerned not only with bias and access, but with which women have the right to speak for, or represent, other women in the policymaking process. To pursue this line of thinking, chapter 3 explores why the founders of CWA and IWF formed themselves into women's organizations and why they consider being women's organizations critical to fulfilling their missions and goals. In many ways, the very existence of CWA and IWF is paradoxical. Both organizations chastise feminists for making identity-based claims on behalf of women. Each has argued that feminists should be discredited for seeking to represent women as a whole, because women are not a homogeneous group. However, like the many feminist interest groups they criticize, CWA and IWF seek to represent women. As such, both employ the tactic of "strategic essentialism,"[18] deploying their "womanhood" selectively to contest feminist claims of representation and to give conservative interests more legitimacy. That is, they act as and for women, even while recognizing the trappings of this strategy.

The second part of the book analyzes issue frames. These chapters evaluate organizational narratives on a number of key women's policy concerns that have been central to feminist organizations' agendas for decades: violence against women, child care, and women's health. These issues work well as points of contrast for two reasons. First, they are common to both organizations, thus allowing direct comparisons. Second, they are issues that have been, or are currently, priorities for national *feminist* organizations and activists. As such, analyses of these topics provide insights into how CWA and IWF directly tackle feminist successes, failures, and goals.

The discourse of interest groups shapes meanings about political interests and accomplishes three critical tasks: providing diagnoses of events and problems in need of alteration; offering proposed solutions to the problems raised; and eliciting calls to arms or rationales for engaging in corrective actions.[19] This discourse has practical implications in terms of policy outcomes as well, since some version of these debates will be translated into public policy and social practices.[20]

CWA and IWF construct issues in ways that position themselves as representatives of women's interests and that mobilize women to support conservative causes. Through analyses of organizational rhetoric, I have located three specific frames that CWA and IWF employ, and I refer to these frames as "antifeminist," "women's interests," and "social/economic conservative." I delineate analyses of IWF's and CWA's rhetoric by these descriptors, but also note when and why the organizations artfully link or juxtapose their messages, producing comprehensive narratives that mediate conservative values through feminist language, or vice versa. By engaging in this "frame transformation," the groups reinterpret opposing or inconsistent values and beliefs through their own narratives and shift the meaning of issues to be more consistent with their views.[21] Here, frame transformation produces language that makes sense of feminist discourse in ways that conservatives recognize and favor. In so doing, CWA and IWF attend to the tension between their conservative beliefs and their need to appeal to women who feel they have benefited from the feminist movement.

Through antifeminist frames, the organizations acknowledge feminist activism on a range of issues, but also chastise their liberal counterparts for misleading women into believing that feminist activism can solve women's problems. CWA and IWF know that feminists have altered the social and political environment, but also recognize that many women shy away from specifically affiliating with the term feminism itself. Perhaps because media have often narrowly and negatively defined feminism and the feminist movement,[22] the phrase elicits adverse reactions from some women. Nonetheless, one survey of women found that 80% reflected positively on the "women's movement" of the past, likely because it opened up economic and educational opportunities for women and pushed for things like pay equity and fair credit for women.[23] Another study concluded that a majority of women believe that the "women's movement" has made their lives better, but only a small percentage of these women consider themselves to be "feminists." These data reflect a clear shift over time: support for the women's movement has increased since the early 1970s, but an increasing group of people view the term *feminist* as an insult.[24] CWA and IWF expertly exploit this tension, calling on their members and other women to join them in making women's lives more meaningful by turning back or turning over what they deem to be "feminist" gains. Since the term feminism itself gets mixed reactions from the public,[25] these organizations invoke the phrase in criticizing public policies and liberal ideologies, often making its meaning more unappealing by adding "radical" as an adjective. In addition, evoking antifeminist sentiment enables CWA and IWF to establish their own identities as women's groups. The organizations hope that this will allow them to demonstrate why their perspectives differ from and are more credible than those of feminists. Through their antifeminist frames, CWA and IWF construct themselves as having the "right" interpretation of problems and offer narratives that reinforce women's uncertainties about feminism and that cast feminists as inadequate representatives of women's interests.

By making use of women's interests frames, the organizations shift feminist definitions of issues like child care and violence against women to conform to their own assessments. CWA and IWF use their narratives to demonstrate that they care about women and have their concerns at heart. Such frames show that, like their feminist counterparts, conservative women can be "gender conscious."[26] Referencing issues in terms of women's interests also disrupts the common conflation of feminism with women.[27] This serves the purpose of defining women's issues in ways that are more palatable to conservatives and broadens what we understand to be conservative issues. When juxtaposed with antifeminist frames, this can be a powerful rhetorical device through which the organizations posit fresh and perhaps more effective-sounding solutions to social and political problems.

Finally, the organizations invoke frames that emanate quite specifically from their distinct ideological foundations. That is, CWA references issues through socially conservative language, while IWF might articulate narratives grounded in economic conservative terms. The employment of words that resonate directly with other social and economic conservatives helps the organizations to bring conservatives to them and to solidify their bases.[28] In addition, it extends the scope of social and economic conservatism to include the issues that CWA and IWF prioritize. In effect, this tactic makes the conservative movement appear more sympathetic to and inclusive of women's interests. It also has the effect of transforming the meaning of conservative politics, by making explicit the centrality of women and women's issues to this movement.

DATA AND METHODS

This book employs a case study method.[29] Unlike methods such as survey research, case studies permit an examination of contextual variables and provide a more nuanced assessment of these organizations.[30] The universe of national conservative women's organizations is relatively small compared to feminist institutions, but it is growing (see chapter 2). CWA and IWF are the most prominent, well established, and prolific of these advocates.[31] As such, analyzing these two organizations allows for more general claims to be made about conservative women's national activism. I gathered data from twenty in-depth interviews with organizational leaders, extensive qualitative data analysis of CWA and IWF publications and Web sites, and participant observation. For a complete description of these data and methods, see appendixes A and B.

UNDERSTANDING CONSERVATIVE WOMEN'S SIGNIFICANCE

Studying the political participation of conservative women organized into interest groups advances our thinking about gender and policymaking. It moves beyond analyses of feminist organizations[32] and feminist political participation[33] to show how ideological differences factor into how we conceptualize women's interests and how we understand the relationship between identity and public policymaking.

When political observers do write about conservative women, they portray these advocates as outside the mainstream of political activity. Sara Diamond[34] suggests that designating conservative groups as extreme obscures the ways that many right-wing activities are "system-supported" and thus profoundly affect policymaking. James Guth and his colleagues support Diamond's findings, noting the increasing politicization of evangelical Protestant groups and their heightened willingness to use traditional lobbying and educational strategies to challenge government policies.[35] Feminists and other liberals have not denied the impact of right-wing movements on feminist goals and activities,[36] but some characterize conservative women as victims of false consciousness, pawns of conservative men,[37] or "women's auxiliar[ies] of the conservative elite."[38] For example, on the subject of "right-wing" women, feminist Andrea Dworkin laments:

> The tragedy is that women so committed to survival cannot recognize that they are committing suicide. The danger is that self-sacrificing women are perfect foot soldiers who obey orders, no matter how criminal those orders are. The hope is that these women, upset by internal conflicts that cannot be stilled by manipulation...will be forced to articulate the realities of their own experiences as women subject to the will of men.[39]

Similarly, gay rights advocate Steven Gardiner writes of CWA: "CWA activists, though they may appear to be showing dangerous signs of independence, are in fact doing the will of their husbands and their Christian duty to promote pro-family values."[40]

For feminists, this negative depiction can be particularly problematic, as any dismissal of conservative women's organizations restricts feminists' ability to fully understand their opponents' successes and how to engage them in an effective manner. It also forecloses understanding of conservative women's political participation and leads to mistaken conclusions and assumptions in feminist explanations of women's policy preferences.

By showing how CWA and IWF frame policies in terms of women's interests and from a women's point of view, this book disrupts the common fusing of feminist and/or liberal with women's interests. For example, some research on gender consciousness and women's policy concerns argues that the "expression of a woman's perspective" with regard to policy preferences is facilitated, in part, by a "feminist identity."[41] Conclusions based on this scholarship cluster conservative women with men, erasing the potential for understanding the distinctively gender-conscious policy preferences among conservative women. And, even when scholars are attentive to the differences between feminist and nonfeminist women, they eventually leave conservative women out of analyses because they are not feminist and presumably act like men. But conservative women are changing public discourse about women's interests; indeed, one of the main goals of IWF is to transform debates about "women's" issues by offering the viewpoints of conservative women. CWA refers to itself as the "nation's largest public policy women's organization." When conservative women leaders act as women to make claims for women, they can undermine feminist claims about political representation. That is, CWA and IWF challenge the notion that organized feminist groups like NOW are the ones that know what women want. And their activism has had, and continues to have, very real political consequences. Even if feminists abhor the efforts of these conservative actors, it is essential that they acknowledge and investigate the role of conservatives in public and legislative debates about women.

In addition to providing insights into how feminist activism is disrupted by conservative women's political participation, this book explores the ways in which women's issues can be understood through the ideological lens of conservatism and how women authorize conservative causes. Conservative women bring different perspectives and motivations than men do to their activism.[42] By acting as women and defining women's interests in ways that differ from feminists and their conservative male counterparts, CWA and IWF expand the scope of what we consider to be conservative values and policy goals, and they provide legitimacy to issue positions that would be dismissed if conservative men were the ones making the political claims.

CWA and IWF can also draw women into conservative campaigns[43] and demonstrate the centrality of female political actors to a movement that has been charged with sexism and with hindering women's social and professional mobility. This is important for a movement that suffers from electoral gender gaps and is prone to public perceptions of hostility toward women's interests.[44] Indeed, the Republican Party has started to recognize the gender gap and the need for conservative women to be more visible. In 2004, the Republican National Committee initiated a "Winning Women" program to get more women involved in leadership positions within the party. George W. Bush's reelection operatives also ran a "W Stands for Women" campaign through which Republican women leaders made appearances around the country, encouraging other women to vote for Bush.

Through their efforts, CWA and IWF make it more difficult for feminists and other liberals to criticize conservatives for not caring about women. When these organizations speak as and for women, they project an image of conservatism that is friendly to women and promote conceptualizations of issues that differ from those of their male counterparts. As such, these conservative women's groups are well positioned to shape public opinion, influence how policymakers think about public issues, and mobilize women to join conservative causes.

LOOKING AHEAD

I begin my analysis in chapter 2 with a brief history of conservative women's political activism, providing context to and continuity with the efforts of CWA and IWF. I also describe the organizations in more detail and discuss their relationship to other conservative organizations and leaders. Chapter 3 explores their representational strategies and documents the extent to which conservative women's organizations rely on the relationship between gender identity and representation to further their missions. It shows why CWA and IWF consider the presence of women in positions of political leadership integral to the construction of their political legitimacy. This translates into their putting forth women to speak to the media and to lobby members of Congress, in part as a foil against the perceived threat of feminist hegemony. These actions emphasize the significance of gender identity to them, even as they scoff at feminists for doing the same. By engaging in tactics they simultaneously impugn, they make evident moments of contradiction but explain these contradictions through the political context in which they operate.

In chapters 4, 5, and 6, I shift gears to examine how CWA and IWF advocate for specific policy goals. Chapter 4 highlights how the organizations address the issue of violence against women. Violence against women has long been a feminist bailiwick, which has received considerable national attention since the passage of the Violence Against Women Act of 1994. So where do conservative women position themselves in terms of this activism? Do they side with feminists and risk alienating their conservative base, or do they oppose feminists and take the chance that they might be perceived as not caring about women? As this chapter shows, both tackle this challenge with similar narratives but to different ends. CWA takes on the issue of pornography and advocates for strict regulation of the industry. Through its discourse, the organization stresses the connections between pornography and violence against women, transforming conservative messages into those consistent with feminist ones—in this case, more prominent discussions of pornography's effects on women overshadow rhetoric about the moral perversion of pornography. IWF takes on two issues: the Violence Against Women Act, arguing that it is a feminist boondoggle and a waste of taxpayers' money; and sexual harassment, claiming that feminists have gone too far in interpreting laws and developing workplace policies. As it interprets the issue of violence against women through economic conservative values, it also argues that its policy goals are in the best interest of women, thus claiming credibility as a women's organization.

Chapter 5 examines organizational rhetoric about motherhood and policies that address the conflict between parenting and the workplace. Both groups position feminists at the heart of women's frustration over family policies and construct conservative images of maternal identities to promote their call for limited government involvement in this area. This analysis also shows how both groups' idealization of motherhood fits well within the parameters of social and economic conservatism and, as such, enables the organizations to be catalysts for fusionism, a tactic that has helped to build the conservative movement. In so doing, the chapter explores the implications of having two prominent conservative women's organizations articulate shared messages and assesses the fluidity of ideological boundaries between social and economic conservatives.

Chapter 6 demonstrates how CWA and IWF articulate issues central to the conservative movement—abortion and scientific research and development—in terms of women's health. By showing how CWA and IWF gender conservative policy priorities, this chapter illuminates the role of women's organizations in constructing the broader conservative movement as one that takes women's interests seriously. Specifically, CWA frames debates about abortion and family planning in terms of their effects on women's physical and emotional well-being, thereby promoting the idea that those opposed to abortion care about women as well as fetuses. This is meant to address critics who charge antiabortion activists with disregarding women's well-being in their quest for making abortion illegal.

As part of its health policy platform, IWF contends that there is too much government intervention in medical and scientific research. Its reasoning emanates from economic principles that call for less regulation of scientific research and development, including those related to the production of pharmaceuticals and medical technologies. But, unlike its economic conservative counterparts, it brings a gendered perspective to these debates by highlighting why these issues should matter to women

I conclude the book, in chapter 7, by discussing how the study of CWA and IWF provides fresh ways of thinking about political representation and identity politics, conservative movements and women's political activism.

By evaluating the significance of CWA and IWF, this book demonstrates the importance of shedding light on these prominent political players. It provides insights into how conservative women leaders think about their work on an individual level and how that translates into organizational strategy and action. In presenting and assessing their own views, and taking them seriously as activists, this book urges that we go beyond seeing conservative women as those who are "subject to the will of men"[45] and recognize the power they have as political actors.

Chapter 2

CONSERVATIVE WOMEN'S POLITICAL ACTIVISM

Women have always organized to contest feminist policies and successes. Groups like the National Association Opposed to Woman Suffrage (NAOWS) and STOP-ERA were run by capable female leaders intent on undermining feminist claims of representation and promoting conservative points of view. Other women have joined conservative organizations like Young Americans for Freedom (YAF)[1] and worked on campaigns to get right-wing candidates elected to office. Although their activities have differed in approaches, goals, and rhetoric, these women have been integral to conservative movement politics. As women who have organized as women to oppose feminist advocacy, they are mostly bound by gender-based visions of maintaining a culture premised on women's social and biological differences from men. Appeals to maternalism are often featured, with women claiming legitimacy as actors through their status as mothers, or by arguing that feminism devalues women's roles as primary caretakers. Many have pitted women against each other through tactics meant to sharpen divisions based on class, race, and/or sexuality. It may be an overstatement to say that there is a conservative women's movement, but there has been sustained activism in the United States by right-leaning women over the years. In the chronological account that follows, I offer some highlights of conservative women's political activism and contrast them with CWA and IWF activism. Here, conservative women's activism is put into historical context, illuminating the efforts of those who have specifically opposed feminism and promoted right-wing causes.

Whatever their particular intent, the advocacy of conservative women has been premised on the idea that feminism is too radical and threatens their preferred gendered order of social relations. More current advocates also claim that feminists have strayed too far from the goal of promoting equality. Over the decades, conservative women have had close male allies in government, business, and advocacy groups, and their work, directly or indirectly, has shaped and bolstered conservative politics broadly speaking. For more than a century, women have been central to conservative politics, providing not only time, energy, and money, but legitimacy as well.

"Woman Suffrage Opposed to Woman's Rights"

The campaign for women's suffrage was protracted and complicated. Of course, it was ultimately successful, and in 1920, women won the right to vote in every state in the nation. Suffragists not only faced opposition from men; they faced it from women as well. It may now seem odd that women would strenuously work to reject such a fundamental right, but fears about the loss of class and racial privilege, fueled by increased levels of immigration, compelled some women to wage a fierce battle to oppose ratification of the Nineteenth Amendment.

The first evidence of women's opposition to suffrage in the United States was documented in 1868, when a group of women fought against a Massachusetts initiative promoting female voting rights.[2] The proposal went nowhere, but both sides continued to mobilize as the push for women's suffrage gained momentum. As the intensity of the battle grew, more women became involved on both sides. The National Association Opposed to Woman Suffrage (NAOWS), headed by Josephine Dodge, represented women who challenged the fight for women's right to vote. Founded in 1911, it peaked at 350,000 members and coordinated activities in twenty-five states. The majority of its leaders and members were women whose husbands were prominent politicians and industrialists, many from elite Eastern states. They were generally wealthy and represented the interests of upper-income society. Gaining significant momentum between 1912 and 1916,[3] NAOWS published the *Woman's Protest* and was credited in part with helping to defeat almost forty woman suffrage referenda in the states.[4] Dodge and others argued that suffrage would undermine women's privileged status and burden them with duties that would detract from their more important and central domestic lives. In a publication devoted to winning the antisuffrage campaign, Dodge wrote:

> It is woman's right to be exempt from political responsibility in order that she may be free to render her best service to the state. The state has surrounded her with protective legislation in order that she may attain her highest efficiency in those departments of the world's work for which her nature and her training fit her.[5]

With views premised on the concept of "separate spheres," these advocates did not necessarily consider women to be unequal to men, but felt that the "sexes [should be] matched in their valuation as to intellectual gifts and oral virtue," which should be applied in distinct fashions.[6] This attention to gender role distinctions meant that women who actively opposed suffrage faced "mobilization dilemmas"[7] because they sought to reaffirm a doctrine that placed women within the domestic realm, while simultaneously engaging in "public" life to do so. To address this tension, female antisuffragists arranged their spaces of activity to look genteel, like parlors, and claimed to be waging "educational" not "political" campaigns.[8]

Like CWA and IWF, antifeminist rhetoric was central to the antisuffragists' cause. They constructed supporters of suffrage as radicals whose efforts would destroy family life, women's status, and the "right of females to lifetime financial support."[9] Ultimately, NAOWS and others failed, in part because they did not establish a coordinated nationwide strategy. This led to weak external support, and suffragists won with a national strategy.[10] Although they were defeated, it is important to recognize the ways in which these astute activists gave credence to antifeminist advocacy.[11] In addition, understanding the work of women opposed to suffrage illuminates the ways in which some women sought, and found, political power and voice during a period when men dominated political and economic life.

Patriots and Guardians of the White Race

After the passage of the Nineteenth Amendment, many suffragists were empowered to continue their political involvement. However, the issue that once united them, women's suffrage, was gone, and women were freer to divide along class, race, and ideological lines.[12] Some moved into Progressive Era politics, engaging in direct service work for poor and immigrant families and working to pass social welfare legislation. Others, however, chose a different route: they opted to participate in racist efforts and organizations, and they were driven by anti-immigrant, white supremacist, and nationalistic ideologies.[13] Some of these women put their efforts into forming Women of the Ku Klux Klan (WKKK), a group that bolstered the terrorist activities of the KKK, but also acted independently by calling on white Protestant women to protect "pure womanhood" and assert their newfound political rights. Many came into WKKK on their own, drawn in neither by their husbands nor by other men. Through WKKK, women organized social events, boycotts, and electoral activities. They argued that the maintenance of racial, ethnic, and religious superiority was central to preserving the American family and women's privileged role within it.[14] They drew on traditional conceptions of maternalism to guard their home life and through their efforts expanded our understanding of what it means to be political. That is, inspired by their gendered roles, these women used events like Klan wedding services and funerals to promote Klan-based ideology and create a "sense of the totality of the Klan World."[15] In so doing, WKKK exemplified the importance of building social networks to maintaining political movements.

During World War II, a smaller, but no less conservative group of women invoked similarly racist and purportedly patriotic appeals to rally against U.S. involvement in the war. This "mothers' movement" promoted isolationism, anti-Semitism, and opposition to New Deal policies.[16] Like other conservative women, these activists were marked by their gender-conscious activism and argued that women should have equal opportunity to participate in politics, but on terms having to do with their motherhood. Ideologically driven, they were less concerned about women ultimately making political gains, but focused on the fact that the wrong men were in charge. They grounded their arguments in maternalist discourse, claiming that "mothers, especially interested in protecting their sons, had to clean out government and bring the proper men to power."[17] They shied away from challenging men's status and instead insisted that women's obligations as wives and mothers required them to challenge U.S. foreign policy.[18]

The postsuffrage era of conservative women's activism saw activists rallying around maternalism, calling on women to extend the notion of motherhood to be about women as guardians of racial purity and public morality. WKKK, for example, promoted the idea of procreation being critical to the survival of the white race, thereby using motherhood to normalize racism.[19] Women in the twenty-first century still participate in extreme right-wing groups,[20] but as Chapter Six will show, more mainstream organizations like CWA and IWF invoke maternalism to foreground discussions of gender differences and to counter feminist advocacy around family and workplace policies.

Women and the Ascendancy of American Conservatism

The growth in American conservatism is often linked to the presidential campaign of Barry Goldwater. Grassroots activists cut their teeth working on his unsuccessful bid to defeat Lyndon B. Johnson in 1964. Before the election, conservatives from around the country started to mobilize in organizations like the John Birch Society and YAF,[21] groups that reflected growing pockets of conservatism in the suburbs and on college campuses. Women were well represented among these political actors and were even overrepresented in the rank and file of a growing conservative movement in southern California.[22] Newly forming Christian Right organizations groomed women like Connie Marshner, who later became active in campaigns to elect Ronald Reagan and other social conservatives to office.[23] Through their involvement in right-wing electoral and mobilization efforts, these women gained important organizing and political skills, enlisted other women, and developed substantial conservative political and social networks. Many applied what they learned through YAF, for example, to organize other women in future political campaigns.[24]

One woman who became prominent during Goldwater's ascendancy is Phyllis Schlafly. With her publication of the widely distributed *A Choice, Not an Echo*,[25] she attacked what she considered to be the narrow and elite Eastern Republican establishment and led a charge to change the focus of the Republican Party and promote Goldwater as well. Klatch documents that Schlafly played an important role in training and encouraging other "traditionalist" women to be politically aware and effective.[26]

Schlafly, a former congressional candidate and Republican Party activist,[27] founded in 1972 the Eagle Forum, an organization she still leads. She is perhaps most famous for having directed the opposition to the Equal Rights Amendment (ERA). Through STOP-ERA, she ran a well-organized, top-down campaign to block passage of the amendment, which would have made sex discrimination explicitly unconstitutional. Appealing to public anxiety over women being drafted and to some women's concerns that men could be absolved of their familial financial commitments, she led one of the most visible and successful antifeminist campaigns in U.S. history,[28] a campaign in which CWA also played an active role. Like the women in this study, Schlafly was well aware of the salience of her gender in this case: having women argue against the ERA gave legitimacy to their stance and allowed men who opposed it to reference women's concerns about its ratification. Active to this day, Schlafly is an icon of conservative women's leadership.

Institutionalizing Antifeminism

This book documents the efforts of two prominent contemporary conservative women's organizations, but there are also others. Since the 1980s, groups like the Women's Freedom Network and Renaissance Women have sprung up, helping to create a solid network of conservative women that spans generations and views about issues like abortion. All of these organizations have at some time worked with either CWA and/or IWF. Two relatively new groups have been inspired by the work of Students for Academic Freedom (SAF) and the Young America's Foundation—organizations that mobilize conservative college students and advance the idea that right-wing views are not tolerated in classrooms by college professors. The Clare Booth Luce Policy Institute (CBLPI), founded in 1993, is committed to principles such as "individual freedom" and sponsors a conservative speakers program that brings women like Ann Coulter to college campuses. It publishes a student guide to assist conservative women in countering Valentine's Day activities that center around the production of the feminist *Vagina Monologues*, because the play "glorifies social deviancy and sexual perversion."[29] It urges women to "reclaim the romance and beauty of Valentine's Day" by organizing alternative campus activities that "celebrate the intellect, strength and integrity and spirit of the modern American woman," and CBLPI has worked with IWF to promote this position.

Like SAF and YAF, the organization condemns women's studies and helps to groom young conservatives to be media darlings. Similarly motivated are the students who formed the Network of Enlightened Women (NeW), a fledgling association created to "foster the education and leadership skills of conservative university women...[and] devoted to expanding the intellectual diversity on college campuses."[30] IWF highlighted the group's efforts by publishing an interview with its founder, Karin Agness, on its Web site and presenting NeW as "an intellectual home for college women who don't blindly follow the herd." Both CBLPI and NeW are part of a larger conservative movement and, like CWA and IWF, hope that being women's organizations will not only challenge feminist claims of representation, but will also bring a young female-friendly face to conservative causes.

On the electoral politics front, some have adopted the EMILY's List approach and founded political action committees to raise money for women candidates. Founded in 1992, WISH List raises money for prochoice Republican women, and its antiabortion counterpart, Susan B. Anthony List, "assists pro-life women candidates and works to defeat proabortion women candidates and incumbents."[31] The seven-decades-old National Federation of Republican Women (NFRW) promotes Republican Party politics and issues. Claiming 100,000 members, the organization runs campaign management schools and recruits Republican women to run for public office. All of these organizations aim to rectify the fact that the entry of Republican women into elective office has lagged behind that of Democratic women and to show the political power of women within the party. As I will discuss in Chapter Three, neither CWA nor IWF devote resources to increasing the number of women elected officials, but both work closely with Republican Party leaders to shape and bolster its goals.

Spokeswomen for Conservatism

Acting in conjunction with conservative organizations are a number of prominent women who have made names for themselves as spokespeople and pundits. Not all of them talk about women's issues per se, but the political significance of their gender does not go unnoticed. Dubbed "conservative chic," women like Ann Coulter, Michelle Malkin, and Laura Ingraham have captured significant media attention and given right-wing politics a female face.[32] CBLPI promotes the importance of these women by publishing a "Great American Conservative Women" calendar, which has featured Ann Coulter, former CWA president Carmen Pate, and IWF advisory board member and U.S. secretary of labor Elaine Chao. Perhaps the most popular of these "great Americans" is Coulter. Known for her miniskirts and outrageous comments (she called women who lost their husbands in 9/11 "a gaggle of weeping widows" whose advocacy efforts were "rabid"),[33] Coulter has published numerous books castigating liberals. In her bestselling *How to Talk to a Liberal (If You Must)*, she includes an essay about feminism that proclaims:

The real reason I loathe and detest feminists is that real feminists, and the core group, the Great Thinkers of the movement, which I had until now dismissed as the invention of a frat boy on a dare, have been at the forefront in tearing down the very institutions that protect women: monogamy, marriage, chastity, and chivalry. And surveying the wreckage, the best they have to offer is: Call me Ms.[34]

She continues, adding that "feminists are also marauding, bloodthirsty vipers."[35] While she includes feminists in her contemptuous rhetoric, Coulter's essays and public appearances are not tailored to directly target feminists. There are other commentators, however, whose careers are more closely defined by their ardent attacks on feminism. Christina Hoff Sommers, for example, published *Who Stole Feminism?* in which she contends that women have been victimized by "gender" feminists—self-interested, elite, privileged actors who pit women against men.[36] In her book, she chastises feminists' alleged preoccupation with pain and oppression and argues that most women are not represented by feminists within the academy or in national organizations. A resident scholar at the conservative American Enterprise Institute (AEI), Sommers has had her research supported by conservative donors like the John M. Olin Foundation. She has worked closely with IWF and gives speeches through CBLPI's speakers series. She has challenged AAUW's report about sex discrimination in schools, charging that AAUW used faulty data, exaggerated its claims, and urged the creation of a "nightmarish 'gender equity' bureaucracy"[37] to ensure that girls are not discriminated against in the public education system. Sommers also argues that young women need to be warned about the radicalism of "new feminists":

American women—as a group—are not oppressed. In fact, they are among the most favored, privileged and blessed group of human beings in the world. To most students, this rings true. But for those who have taken a lot of "feminist theory" or who are heavily involved with the campus "Take Back the Night"/Vagina Monologues culture, those are fighting words. They insist they are oppressed and resent the suggestion they are not. So there is still some hissing and booing—and, these days, angry text messaging among feminists in the audience.[38]

Scholars like Daphne Patai and Elizabeth Fox-Genovese have joined with Sommers to attack women's studies and the supposed liberal bias of academia in general. Both Sommers and Fox-Genovese have been embraced by IWF and have served on its national advisory board. When Fox-Genovese died in January 2007, she was eulogized by IWF as being an "independent woman" with "intellectual courage."[39]

For more than a century, women have organized for antifeminist and conservative causes. As women's political clout grows, and as these particular activists continue to institutionalize their work, we should expect to see a conservative women's movement in formation. For conservatives, this is good news, but for feminists it means the necessity to clarify and specify movement claims, and requires accounting for women who take issue with feminist policies and goals. The following provides details about the two prominent conservative women's organizations under study here and explains their relationship with other conservative groups. The stability of both organizations is notable, and both are poised to lead this growing movement of conservative women's organizations and leaders.

THE ORGANIZATIONS

See tables A and B for an overview of these organizations and their priorities.

CWA, IWF, and Conservative Movement Politics

The formation of CWA and IWF coincided with two distinct periods of intense right-wing mobilization and political power in the United States. Although the organizations are effective and influential in their own right, they also work closely with other conservative organizations, individuals, and policymakers. They frequently reference these allies in their work to show that other "experts" and professionals agree with their positions. For example, CWA cites Baruch College biology professor Joel Brind when arguing for restrictions on abortion. As will be detailed later, Brind published a study claiming that abortion causes breast cancer.

In spite of their significance, some have discounted conservative women as being co-opted by conservative men and for having political connections to other conservatives.[40] For example, the liberal watchdog group Media Transparency says that IWF is neither *independent* nor a *forum*, arguing that it merely "serves up women who mouth the conservative movement party line."[41] While this section places CWA and IWF in the context of other conservative political actors, it is

TABLE A. Overview of Organizations

	Concerned Women for America (CWA)	Independent Women's Forum (IWF)
Year Founded	1979	1992
Stated Mission[a]	The mission of CWA is to protect and promote biblical values among all citizens—first through prayer, then education, and finally by influencing our society—thereby reversing the decline in moral values in our nation.	IWF's mission is to rebuild civil society by advancing economic liberty, personal responsibility, and political freedom. IWF fosters greater respect for limited government, equality under the law, property rights, free markets, strong families, and a powerful and effective national defense and foreign policy. IWF is home to the next wave of the nation's most influential scholars—women who are committed to promoting and defending economic opportunity and political freedom.
Number of Members	500,000[b]	20,337[c]
Annual Budget[d]	$8,085,000	$1,045,000
Ideology	Social Conservative	Economic Conservative
Major Source of Funds	Membership dues; Grewcock Foundation; U.S. Department of Justice; royalties from book sales	Foundations (Scaife, Roe, Bradley, Earhart, Castle Rock, Shelby Cullom Davis, Jaquelin Hume, Gilder, Donner, Randolph, JM, Peters, Olin); individual contributions; U.S. Department of Justice

[a]Statements can be found on the organizations' Web sites: www.cwfa.org and www.iwf.org, respectively.
[b]As reported by CWA; this is the number of people who have ever been members.
[c]As reported to me by IWF staff member Stacy Chin on November 20, 2006; one may become an associate or student member by filling out a form on the IWF's Web site. Of the 20,337 members, 1,812 are student members.
[d]As reported on 2004 IRS Form 990 under "contributions, gifts, grants and similar amounts received."

TABLE B. Overview of CWA and IWF Issue Priorities (2007)

Concerned Women for America	Independent Women's Forum
Pornography (restricting access to pornography; opposition to sex trafficking in women; supporting laws regulating child pornography)	Violence against Women (opposition to provisions in VAWA)
Sanctity of Life (opposition to legal abortion, most forms of birth control, and stem cell research)	Health/Science (challenging environmentalists; arguing for attention to biological differences between women and men in research; opposition to precautionary principle; supporting tort reform)
National Sovereignty/International Issues (opposition to funding of United Nations and to ratifying CEDAW)	International Women's Issues/ National Security (rights for women in Iraq and Afghanistan; opposition to ratifying CEDAW; support of war in Iraq)
Education (promoting abstinence-based education and support for home schooling)	Education (mobilizing women on campuses to challenge feminist professors; opposition to Title IX; opposition to affirmative action; advocating for research on boys in schools)
Definition of Family (opposing same-sex marriage and other rights for gays and lesbians; promoting married heterosexual families)	Family/Workplace (promoting flex time; privatizing Social Security; arguing against gender-based wage gaps and federal funding of child care; opposing use of hostile environment claims in sexual harassment cases)
Religious Liberty (advocating school prayer; supporting teaching of intelligent design; faith-based advocacy)	

important to emphasize that I disagree with the characterization of CWA and IWF as mere mouthpieces. Chastising conservative women for their relationship to powerful conservatives undermines women's political power and agency. Unless we believe they are expressing their political concerns and opinions under duress, it is critical to consider them on their own terms. Of course, seeing where they fit in the scheme of movement politics is essential to understanding the sources of their power, members, and legitimacy, but it should not be used to dismiss them. Indeed, the closeness of IWF and CWA to conservative leaders, organizations, and donors reinforces how central and relevant these organizations are to contemporary politics.

CWA has been a key player in conservative evangelical politics and is one of the most enduring religious right groups of the past three decades.[42] CWA's founder, Beverly LaHaye, is married to Tim LaHaye, well known for his efforts in mobilizing Christian Right activities in the late 1970s and early 1980s. Together, they published in 1976 *The Act of Marriage*, a book targeted to married evangelical Christian couples to help them learn about sex and sexual gratification. The book was updated and rereleased in 1998.[43] Tim LaHaye is also the coauthor of the bestselling *Left Behind* fictional book series that chronicles evangelical views about the last days on earth before the rapture. Both are strong supporters of other religious right groups and leaders. For example, in 2001, the LaHayes donated $4.5 million to Jerry Falwell's Liberty University;[44] Beverly LaHaye is also a trustee of the university. When Falwell died in May 2007, she bemoaned losing a "long time dear friend."[45] CWA has worked closely over the years with the Moral Majority, which saw its heyday in the 1980s, and with the Christian Coalition, a group that was partly responsible for helping Republicans to reassert electoral power in the 1990s. Currently, CWA works in coalition with a number of prominent antiabortion and anti–gay rights organizations. New Right entrepreneur Paul Weyrich is noted as a "personal friend" of Beverly LaHaye,[46] and popular conservative personalities like Laura Schlesinger (Dr. Laura) and Robert Bork have been honored by CWA.

For its part, IWF aligns itself with conservative organizations like the American Enterprise Institute and receives substantial financial support from donors well known for their advocacy of other conservative movement activities (see table A). Its board and affiliated advisors read like a who's who in conservative politics. The founding executive director, Barbara Ledeen, is married to Michael Ledeen, a former

Reagan appointee and now advisor to Karl Rove. Past and current board members include the late conservative television commentator Barbara Olson, Wendy Lee Gramm, former Reagan administration economist and wife of U.S. senator Phil Gramm (R-TX), and American Enterprise Institute scholar Christina Hoff Sommers. Since its inception, IWF has honored people like Ward Connerly, a well-known African American who successfully spearheaded a campaign to ban affirmative action in California, and former Republican House Speaker Newt Gingrich. Talk-show host and conservative political commentator Laura Ingraham helped the organization in its formative years and remains on its national advisory board. High-profile right-wing pundit Ann Coulter has been deemed by IWF to be among the "women we love." IWF often holds public events that feature conservative lawmakers, writers, and advocates. In 2007, for example, it hosted an evening dedicated to "helping your child love this country" with former *Ladies' Home Journal* editor Myrna Blyth and presidential speechwriter Chriss Winston.

With support and attention from George W. Bush's administration, both organizations continue to build alliances with other like-minded activists. For example, during President Bush's tenure in office, both CWA and IWF have received federal funds from the U.S. State Department. CWA won a grant to hold a conference on sex trafficking, and IWF was awarded money to help the "promotion of women's full political and economic participation in Iraq."[47] Such affirmation not only helps to sustain the organizations, but provides them with legitimacy as well.

While both are considered part of the conservative movement broadly speaking, a salient distinction between the organizations is the religiosity of the CWA. IWF is leery of CWA's evangelical roots, and its support for policies like school prayer and antiabortion laws violates IWF's more secular values. Conversely, at least one interviewee from CWA bemoans IWF's refusal to address issues like abortion and homosexuality.[48] Clearly, this will impact the extent to which they will coalesce. It has not stopped them from working together on a few issues, like opposition to gender integration in the military, but such differences will keep the organizations from becoming too cozy. However, as some of their goals and policy priorities do overlap, they may work together in the future. Chapter 5 addresses this possibility in more detail. The following provides more details about the organizations, focusing on their founding missions and legislative priorities.

Concerned Women for America (CWA) was founded in San Diego in 1979 by Beverly LaHaye, a mother of four who used to organize marriage seminars with her husband. Along with its 500,000 members, the organization employs approximately thirty national staff and boasts an $8 million annual budget. It has a diverse funding base (see table A), which has been considered a contributing factor to its longevity.[49] Its founding was initially spurred by LaHaye's desire to oppose the ERA and to contest feminist claims of representing women. Indeed, its strong objection to feminist activism on behalf of women is clearly articulated in the information it sends to its new and potential members:

> LaHaye watched a television interview with Betty Friedan, founder of the National Organization for Women. Realizing that Betty claimed to speak for the women of America, Mrs. LaHaye was stirred to action. She knew the feminists' anti-God, anti-family rhetoric did not represent her beliefs, or those of the vast majority of women.[50]

The organization's launch and subsequent growth coincided with the politicization of the Christian Right in the late 1970s and early 1980s.[51] At that time, social conservatives were avidly mobilizing to oppose legalized abortion, homosexuality, and communism and to promote school prayer. Leaders like Jerry Falwell ably convinced conservative evangelicals to politicize their religious commitments. As Robert Wuthnow argues, the time was right for such mobilization to occur. In the mid- to late 1970s, criticism of the Vietnam War, legislative responses to Watergate, and U.S. Supreme Court decisions on issues like abortion meant that "morality came to be viewed as a public issue rather than in strictly private terms."[52] The election of an evangelical—Jimmy Carter—to the White House also gave prominence and visibility to those who identified with this religious tradition. Wuthnow argues that, for conservative evangelicals during this time, it felt "sensible" to become politically engaged and to promote their views on morality. As the symbolic line between morality and politics blurred, conservative evangelicals "were no longer speaking as a sectarian group, but as representative[s] of values that were in the interest of all."[53] Under the leadership of activists like Richard Viguerie, religious right groups became familiar with, and adept at using, the latest communication, fundraising, and organizing techniques to rally constituents. Direct-mail appeals containing "alarmist" messages about the evil effects of legal abortion and homosexuality startled and ultimately activated people.[54] These religiously committed individuals had solid, close-knit social and church-based networks that also enabled effective mobilization,[55] especially when local pastors used the pulpit to give political direction to their members. Constituents were encouraged to boycott media outlets that offended their moral sensibilities, and fundamentalist ministers were recruited into politics by leaders like Ed McAteer.[56] As we moved into the 1980s, acceptance from public figures like Ronald Reagan also helped to solidify the evangelicals' base.[57] With a tight and effective infrastructure, large mass-mailing databases, and major media outlets like the Christian Broadcasting Network (CBN), they became a formidable political movement of which CWA was and is a major player.[58]

As a religiously based organization that opposes abortion and homosexuality, CWA is a social conservative interest group.[59] Today, CWA has a professionally staffed office in Washington, DC, claims members in all fifty states, and professes to be the largest women's organization in the United States.[60] Although this book emphasizes how CWA frames its issue debates, the organization employs a host of tactics to effect political change. As I will discuss, this is also true of IWF. Most groups with a presence in Washington, DC, directly lobby members of Congress, testify at hearings, and hold public events like conferences and brown bag lunches. CWA and IWF are no exceptions. CWA has professional and volunteer lobbyists and boasts that its efforts get noticed by legislators. For example, it worked with Representative John Hostettler (R-IN) to introduce the Marriage Protection Act in 2004, a bill that would have disallowed federal legal challenges to the Defense of Marriage Act, a law that says that no state has to recognize another's same-sex marriage. CWA claims to have recruited almost all of the bill's forty-eight House cosponsors and cites Representative Hostettler as saying: "I firmly believe that the support, prayers and hard work of Concerned Women for America's staff and members were critical in the passage of the Marriage Protection Act. Your voice was heard!"[61] Passed in the House, the bill ultimately faltered in the Senate. While it was disheartened by the outcome, CWA did proudly claim one important victory—it had received public recognition from a member of Congress.

Building on the successful techniques used by Viguerie and others to mobilize conservative evangelicals in the 1970s, CWA continuously adapts new technology to get its message out and to attract new members. It broadcasts audio and visual materials over the Internet, offers podcasts and e-alerts, and frequently updates its polished and professional-looking Web site. Its Web site also offers interactive links to enable people to contact local media and their elected officials. Its e-alerts contain fundraising appeals and provide links that easily enable recipients to donate online with the use of a credit card.

Because of CWA's large membership, its strength lies in part in its grassroots. The ability to communicate with and mobilize these adherents is essential for effective lobbying and public education campaigns. Through e-mail, periodicals like *Family Voice*, and its online broadcasts and Web site, its national staff work closely with the grassroots members to update them on legislative affairs and educate them to be activists. Although IWF has a more active strategy of engaging college students, CWA does host a competitive "Ronald Reagan memorial" internship program that enables young women and men to work with the group. Locally, its mostly white[62] female members gather in prayer chapters (650 throughout the United States) to take action on CWA's political agenda. These local prayer groups are the backbone of CWA, providing the organization with an extensive and active nationwide network of women eager to take action on social conservative issues. For example, CWA sponsors the "encourage-a-legislator" program, whereby members are asked to let elected officials know that CWA activists are praying for them. Its national office coordinates volunteers for its Project 535—a group of Washington, DC, area women who meet monthly to canvass lawmakers on issues of concern to the organization (the number 535 refers to the total members of the U.S. Congress). In 2007, for example, women urged legislators to oppose the use of federal funds for stem cell research. Through Project 535, women are trained to lobby, and new members are paired with seasoned activists as they walk the halls of Congress.

In addition to its lobbying and grassroots efforts, CWA houses the Beverly LaHaye Institute (BLI), a think tank devoted to publishing reports and assessing data on topics like abortion and motherhood. Janice Shaw Crouse, a former public relations professional and speechwriter for President George H. W. Bush, heads up the institute. To publicize its views, BLI produces "data digests," semiannual briefs that evaluate research findings to promote its views. For example, in "Abortion: America's Staggering Hidden Loss," Crouse uses figures and charts from the Centers for Disease Control to highlight cases in which abortions are increasing and/or decreasing. In a tragic tone, she notes that the number of women who obtain repeat abortions is increasing, but also celebrates that the total number of abortions in the United States is declining.[63] In a similar vein, CWA works through its Culture and Family Issues unit to produce papers and reports that warn against homosexuality. Both are public education venues, established to offer alternatives to liberal and feminist think tanks like the prochoice Alan Guttmacher Institute (AGI). Unlike BLI, however, AGI conducts primary research on its topics of concern.

Another way for interest groups to have an impact is to form political action committees and raise money for those running for elected office. Because of its nonprofit status, CWA itself cannot directly endorse candidates, but under the name of Beverly LaHaye, it established the Concerned Women Political Action Committee (CWPAC) to allow CWA supporters a more direct voice in electoral outcomes. CWPAC distributed $127,000 in 2005 to candidates that support "conservative principles, values and integrity."[64] It is important to note the central role that religion plays in this organization; conservative evangelical religious beliefs clearly unite and mobilize many of the organization's members and leaders.[65] Its stated mission, to "protect and promote Biblical values among all citizens—first through prayer, then education and finally by influencing our society—thereby reversing the decline in moral values in our nation,"[66] exemplifies its theological convictions. However, as this study documents, CWA, like so many other Christian Right groups, has tailored many of its policy debates to reflect more mainstream concerns and rhetoric.[67] And, what is unique about CWA is that the organization does so in ways meant to establish itself as a serious women's organization.

Its multi-issue policy agenda indicates the full extent of CWA's political participation and is delineated by the following areas of interest: "Definition of the Family," which includes opposition to homosexuality and the promotion of heterosexual marriage; "Sanctity of Life," a platform mostly dedicated to opposing legalized abortion in the United States and abroad; "Education," including supporting curriculum that encourages sexual abstinence; "Pornography," which it opposes; "Religious Liberty," which refers to its belief that expressions of Christianity are wrongly and institutionally obstructed; and "National Sovereignty," which includes opposition to funding the United Nations for fear that it undermines the United States' autonomy. A seventh "Miscellaneous" category encompasses issues that do not neatly fall into the other six (such as taking a position in favor of impeaching President Bill Clinton). Through advocacy on these issues, CWA works in coalition with such conservative organizations as the American Family Association, the Family Research Council, Focus on the Family, and myriad antiabortion groups.

In July 1991, President George Bush nominated Judge Clarence Thomas for a position on the U.S. Supreme Court. Partly because of his conservatism, and partly because he was accused of sexual harassment by his colleague Anita Hill, this nominee—a conservative African-American man—sparked a nasty and prolonged national debate about judicial activism, racism, and sexism. The coalition to oppose his nomination included many feminist organizations, including NOW, AAUW, and the National Women's Law Center. But on the other side stood a group of women rallying behind him: Women for Judge Thomas. Former Thomas colleague and friend Ricky Silberman (who served as IWF's board president) related this story to me about the women who supported Thomas:

> So we devised a strategy...whereby we brought together this group of women from all over the country. And we were the Women for Judge Thomas. What we were going to do, and what we did do, was whenever there was a break in the hearings, and remember Anita Hill had not been heard of at this time. But whenever there was a break in the hearings, we would go out and grab the microphone, and we would put our spin on things....It was incredibly successful in the first set of hearings. The fact that Anita Hill surfaced, I believe, was a result of the fact that Clarence was absolutely on his way to being overwhelmingly approved. There are many people who say part of the reason that was true is we had these women out there saying this guy was the father of sexual harassment law at the EEOC. There are all of these things that he did for women, and he is terrific....It was important that women were saying it, because the fight was going to come primarily from women.[68]

Silberman's recounting of the events highlights IWF's view of the importance of having women speak for conservative causes, an idea which will be elaborated upon in Chapter Three. Although Women for Judge Thomas disbanded after his successful appointment, its leaders were energized by their collective activism against feminism and eventually organized with another group, WIN, the Women's Information Network,[69] to found IWF in 1992. Silberman, a former vice chair and commissioner of the Equal Employment Opportunity Commission, was a pivotal figure in the establishment of IWF.[70] These conservative women leaders are well connected to, or are themselves, key policy and opinion makers. Resembling more of a think tank than a grassroots organization, IWF was founded to take on the "old feminist establishment."[71] Silberman also shared this information about the group's origins:

> They were a bunch of women who were not radical feminists, who didn't want to belong to NOW, because that was so liberal and Democratic. But they also didn't want to belong to CWA, because...for them abortion was not the single overriding issue. Some of them were pro-life, some pro-choice, they were conservative but were not, what we like to call or what I like to call, red meat conservatives. In other words, I think and I continue to think that this was a very mainstream group, but it was a right center as opposed to left center group...but it was very definitely a centrist group of women who didn't belong in NOW and who had no home.[72]

In 1992, the year IWF came into existence, conservative congressional representative Newt Gingrich (R-GA) was also gaining political prominence and power. Through his ardent efforts to undermine Democrats and liberals, he became House Speaker when the Republicans took control of the U.S. Congress in 1994. In this capacity, he fervently pushed his conservative manifesto—the Contract with America—creating a climate conducive for the growth, efficacy, and credibility of the fledgling IWF.

The organization shows no signs of slowing down. It has matured from an organization that was more a "cult of personality" when run by two former staff, Barbara Ledeen, who once worked under Ronald Reagan in the Department of Defense, and Anita Blair, a lawyer who is now a deputy assistant secretary of the navy, to one that has an active board, tight political connections, and regular financial contributions from foundations and individuals. As compared to CWA, IWF is a much younger and smaller organization, but, as Chapter Three will show, it continues to garner considerable media attention. After examining its relationship with conservative leaders and financiers, one scholar concluded that IWF is a "valuable component of the Right's political infrastructure."[73] When George W. Bush became president, his staff contacted IWF, asking for names of potential female appointees.[74] This turned out to be fruitful for IWF, as under Bush, board member Elaine Chao became the U.S. secretary of labor, IWF president Nancy Pfotenhauer was appointed to the UN Commission on the Status of Women and to the Department of Justice's National Advisory Committee on Violence against Women, and national advisory board member Pat Ware served on the Presidential Advisory Council on HIV/AIDS.

IWF is founded on economic conservative principles—believing in free-marketplace ideals and limited federal government involvement in social and economic affairs. It supports tax cuts and incentives for businesses as ways to effect social change. To that end, it claims on its Web site to provide a "voice for American women who believe in individual freedom and personal responsibility...the voice of reasonable women with important ideas who embrace common sense over divisive ideology." When asked how it differs from feminist organizations, one IWF leader also described the group as libertarian:

> I am sure there is more than one, but there is a fairly big one between IWF and the Feminist Majority. It would be almost a government viewed as safety net versus—and women need help because they've been downtrodden in the past—versus kind of a government frequently gets in the way of women's achievements, and we can accomplish anything so long as we are given a shot.... [I]f I had to ascribe a political party name to it, because people like a shorthand, it is like a traditional Democratic versus more of a Libertarian approach.[75]

As this book will show, IWF is not an ideal type when it comes to economic conservatism, but it stays fairly true to its ideological foundations. In the moments where it meshes economic with social conservatism, it does not lose stature or legitimacy so much as it offers insights into how conservatism can be complicated and complex.

IWF employs about ten professional staff members in Washington, DC, and operates on an approximately $1.1 million annual budget. It gears itself toward public education through having its leaders make frequent media appearances, publishing research and reports, and sponsoring open forums with well-known conservatives like Newt Gingrich. It also holds day-long conferences for the public and lawmakers on its issue priorities and organizes brown bag lunches around topics such as "Is Nancy Pelosi Really Good for Women?" To raise money and generate publicity, IWF hosts the Barbara K. Olson Women of Valor Award Dinner. Olson was a conservative pundit, founder of IWF, and wife of former U.S. solicitor general Theodore Olson. She was killed in one of the planes that crashed on September 11, 2001. In her honor, IWF presents awards to activists and political leaders, such as Secretary of State Condoleezza Rice. These tactics help IWF to raise both money and awareness of its efforts. In addition, IWF sends out direct-mail appeals to highlight its efforts and generate donations.

Like CWA, IWF employs new technology and forms of communication to interact with constituents and the public. Its "IWF Inkwell" is a daily blog written by staff on issues ranging from energy policy to Hillary Clinton to motherhood. It sends regular e-mails to subscribers alerting them to leaders' media appearances, current issue debates, and upcoming events, and it offers podcasts as well.

Although IWF does not have grassroots members, it does have a growing campus initiative that seeks to mobilize young, college-educated women. It aims to gain adherents through negative constructions of feminist ideology and by promoting the notion that conservatism, while positive, is under siege on college campuses:

> The opportunity for college students to gain a balanced education has become increasingly rare. Students across the country are clamoring for the chance to have an open debate with their peers and professors on the issues that matter to their generation. Instead of wallowing in the idea that women are victims, women on college campuses want to know what to expect when they enter the workforce upon graduation. They need, and deserve, an environment on campus that cultivates and champions personal responsibility instead of depending on victimology as a crutch.[76]

These themes are also featured on IWF's "Campus Corner" Web site link, where articles are posted by, and solicited from, young women about a range of topics, including dating, feminism, and politics. IWF also sponsors an annual college essay contest for female undergraduates; its 2007 competition asked students to answer the following: "what role should 'women's issues' play in the 2008 elections and how do you define women's issues?" In addition, it offers for downloading a "student activist" guide for women who feel there is no place for them "at the feminist table."[77] Seeing that young women have been responding to its message and recognizing that conservative college-based groups like NeW and CBLPI are starting to gain attention, IWF has identified a constituency for itself and the conservative movement more broadly. Along with conservatives like David Horowitz who criticize universities as being too left-wing, IWF warns against those faculty and school officials who are indoctrinating "today's young women on campus with their liberal rhetoric."[78] To address this concern, it started a conservative scholar program to bring in young women as junior fellows to work at IWF over the summer.

IWF adds an antifeminist twist to its advocacy by juxtaposing its anti–"big government" views with narratives about how federal funds are being used to promote feminism. Indeed, conservative movement critic Jean Hardisty keenly describes the IWF's style as "in-your-face . . . that rests on an assumption of a very smart and competent 'us' sticking it to the feminists."[79] By not only being a women's organization that represents economic conservative views, but by also showing that women's issues can be understood through this ideological lens, the organization has created an important niche for itself among conservatives.

IWF also delights in caricaturing feminists and "debunking" supposed myths about issues such as the need for an Equal Rights Amendment and pay equity policies. Its issues generally fall into one of the following programmatic categories: "Family/Workplace," which challenges feminist claims about women's and men's pay differentials and other workplace issues; the previously discussed "Education" component through which IWF reaches out to college women and aims to provide them with an alternative to "rigid feminist orthodoxy"; "Health/Science," which includes initiatives that challenge such "myths" as the correlation between breast implants and connective tissues diseases; and "International Women's Issues/National Security" projects through which it advocates for gender segregation in military training, opposes the Convention on the Elimination of All Forms of Discrimination against Women (CEDAW) on the grounds that the treaty promotes intrusion into other countries, and in its newest enterprise, supported by federal funds, works with women in Iraq to spread its version of democracy throughout that country. To advocate for these issues, IWF has collaborated with other conservative organizations such as the American Enterprise Institute, Center for Equal Opportunity, and Foundation for Academic Standards and Tradition. In addition, IWF has gained publicity by aligning itself with self-proclaimed feminists who mock high-profile women's issues such as date rape and malign women's studies programs.[80]

As members of a larger community of like-minded activists and political institutions, these women's groups fill an important gap in the conservative movement. And it was with that intention that CWA and IWF formed into women's organizations, as I will document in the chapter that follows.

Chapter 3

PLAYING "FEMBALL"
CWA and IWF as Women's Organizations

A S ORGANIZATIONS COMPETING with feminists over the right to make representational claims about women, CWA and IWF must position themselves as credible arbiters of women's interests. As women opposed to the goals of feminist organizations, these conservative women leaders would thus seem justified in establishing women's groups to oppose feminist activism. But IWF speaks critically of politics based on a group's identity. It generally considers appeals to group-based claims antithetical to individual self-sufficiency and progress—values that are central to its economic conservatism. And, although evangelical Protestant women like those of CWA have a history of activism based on their identities as women, mothers, and/or evangelical Protestants,[1] their organizing into a professional, well-staffed national women's organization seems to belie their call for women to prioritize traditional gender roles. Both organizations also repeatedly criticize feminists for making identity-based representational claims as and for women, a strategy that both groups employ.

So why have these women organized into national women's advocacy groups? How does CWA's and IWF's status as women's organizations shape the strategies they use to counter feminists and establish themselves as legitimate representatives of women's interests? How does the need to attend to competing constituencies factor into their founding missions and goals? This chapter turns to these questions by examining how CWA and IWF invoke gender identity. In this context, *gender identity* refers to the organization's specific contentions that women's voices should be heard in debates about political interests and that women's differences from men matter politically. The leaders and staff of CWA and IWF see their organizations as the ones who truly speak to and for women. But, since the spokespeople for CWA and IWF are not elected like most public officials, they need to establish their legitimacy as representatives in other ways. That is, they need effective strategies that emphasize their ability to act for women. To this end, the groups deploy their "womanhood" selectively, but with purpose, to convey to the public, policymakers, their members, and the media that they are the real thing—activists who truly know what women need and are the rightful delegates for women's interests.

As I detailed in chapter 1, to fully understand the strategies that CWA and IWF employ to establish legitimacy as representatives for women, attention to a number of intervening factors is critical. For these conservative political actors, being women's organizations does not come without some tension. Both must contend with competing public influences and audiences. As such, there are moments when their acting collectively as women comes into conflict with their own or their allies' conservative values. Since it is important for both organizations to maintain good working relationships with other conservative organizations and their own conservative members, this struggle looms large. Specifically, what becomes evident from investigating CWA's and IWF's representational strategies is the dissonance between their conservative critiques of identity politics and their simultaneous embracing of identity-based claims. Both CWA and IWF refer to themselves as "women's" organizations. And each repudiates the interests and goals brought forth by another group of women: feminists. In so doing, these groups contest the validity of feminists to make identity-based political claims while simultaneously reinforcing the value of this practice. By disparaging feminists, CWA and IWF challenge feminists' ability to fully know and represent the interests of all women, thus disputing the right of a group to speak for all of its members. On the other hand, as women's organizations themselves, CWA and IWF make gendered identity claims about *their* interests and goals. Similarly, like feminists, these organizations believe that there are situations where it is better to have women present politically to represent other women.

These tensions are never actually resolved, but reflect organizational attempts to negotiate between the goals of their conservative ideologies and critiques of feminists, with the more practical need to engage in identity politics to counteract their opponents. This is especially true for IWF, which is more critical of identity politics than is CWA. At times, however, the end result of having to mediate among these competing needs is paradoxical and inconsistent organizational behavior. Since feminists have attempted to dismiss the efforts of these conservative women's groups on the grounds that they do not present coherent and convincing advocacy strategies, it is important to have insights into why they act as they do. It is also critical to assess the impact of their actions, be they seemingly logical or not, on feminist and conservative politics. In the following discussion, I place the organizations' actions in a theoretical context, exploring debates about identity politics and foregrounding the subsequent substantive analysis.

GENDER IDENTITY AND POLITICAL ACTIVISM

For interest groups like CWA and IWF, engaging in identity politics means making claims on behalf of women; that is, it means representing them. The strategy of invoking gender identity to make representational claims is not without its critics, most of whom are scholars studying and writing about political movements. Judith Butler, for example, argues that identity categories are never merely descriptive but always normative and, as such, exclusionary. She cautions that when "the category of women is invoked as describing the constituency for which feminism speaks, an internal debate invariably begins over what the descriptive content of that term will be."[2] Women of color, poor and working-class women, and lesbians have long argued for attention to diversity within feminist movements and have criticized deploying the category "woman" to make universal claims without regard to the differences that exist among women.[3] Identity politics, these critics contend, runs the risk of assuming that all women have a "true essence—that which is most irreducible, unchanging, and therefore constitutive of a given person or thing,"[4] that is, that such politics are "essentialist." In this context, the term *essentialism* also refers to the notion that women as a group share the same political interests and expect similar policy solutions from lawmakers.

There are scholars, however, who want to retain some version of identity politics, but call for more careful attention to its effects, purposes, and processes.[5] Gayatri Spivak's ideas have often been consolidated under the phrase "strategic use of essentialism."[6] Spivak calls for deconstructing identity categories but adds that deconstruction should be a critique, not a rejection of an identity politics that relies on potentially essentializing categories. She clarifies that "[a] strategy suits a situation; a strategy is not a theory"[7] and thus argues for attention to how particular identity categories are deployed in specific political situations. Collective activism as women, then, requires critical engagement that recognizes the shortcomings of such a strategy, as well as vigilance about its consequences and outcomes.

Spivak's evaluation of the strategic use of essentialism provides important insights that help to explain why CWA and IWF have opted to engage in some level of identity politics, even though they criticize feminists for doing the same. Throughout these pages, I will show that both organizations, but especially IWF, invoke gender identity critically and self-consciously to legitimate conservative values and policies and to contest feminist political activism. They have organized as women to speak for women, and CWA, more so than IWF, stresses its belief in the existence of distinctly gendered interests when justifying its need to engage in identity politics. Of course, these conservative women's organizations risk falling into the same essentializing tendencies as feminists when they make claims as and for women. For example, rarely does either organization talk about racial or class differences among women in general, or even within its own membership. However, both strongly contend that the strategic use of gender identity enables them to contest feminists' claims of representing women's interests—a goal central to their respective missions.

PLAYING FEMBALL: ORGANIZING AS WOMEN

Feminists have demonstrated the success of collective action by organizing as women to achieve political goals. Following feminists' lead, CWA and IWF argue that, to legitimately challenge feminists, they too must make claims as women. That is, they must engage in identity politics. For example, leaders from both organizations are firm in their conviction that, to counter feminism, they had to form into national women's organizations as feminists have done. Anita Blair, cofounder of IWF, acknowledges this strategic use of gender identity with the interesting use of a sports metaphor: "we strongly believed and believe today that women are not a political interest group," but then she notes that "in this credentialist age...there's a game going on and the other side fielded a team and we didn't."[8] She argues that feminists are playing "femball,"[9] and in order for IWF to compete, it has to act according to the terms established by the team that got there first—feminists. IWF's Sally Satel summarizes this sentiment most succinctly: "I see IWF as largely a reactive group. If it weren't for the feminists, it wouldn't exist."[10] Clearly, IWF recognizes the value of acting as women, even if it does so begrudgingly. Although its leaders and associates may prefer to engage politically through other non-gender-identified conservative organizations, it acknowledges that feminists have made great strides by voicing their political concerns collectively as women. Given these considerations, it argues, it makes sense to do the same.

Like IWF, CWA was born to compete with feminists generally and with NOW specifically. CWA New Jersey state leader and local anti-abortion activist Seriah Rein argues that "it is in the public's interest to maintain our identity as a women's organization and as a counterpoint to what NOW is doing specifically."[11] She also adds that because "NOW has been seriously co-opted by the lesbian fringe," CWA provides a welcome home for men who wish to support the efforts of a women's organization. Likewise, CWA staff member Kenda Bartlett relates:

> They hear the Patricia Irelands, the Eleanor Smeals, the Kate Michelmans, all of them saying we represent women in America, what American women think. And these women are saying this is not what I believe and not what I think...so they have looked for a place where they can get information that states their point of view, and they have found that in CWA.[12]

The clarity with which both CWA and IWF express their reasons for forming into women's organizations indicates how centrally the organizations believe that gender identity matters in terms of their founding missions and structures. Other conservative groups may exist to oppose liberal policy agendas, but those that are distinctively women's groups can mesh identity and interest activism in ways that uniquely shape conservative politics.

Beyond being women's organizations in and of themselves, these organizations also produce narratives to construct themselves as the women's organizations that truly represent most women. Both organizations make assertions that go beyond the scope of the people affiliated with their groups, despite the fact that they criticize feminists for doing the same. Each claims to be speaking for those women whom feminists do not represent, which is, according to them, a majority of women. Such discourse positions the organizations in opposition to feminists, as CWA and IWF argue that feminists really only speak for a handful of misguided women. For example, an IWF board member shared that she and other women founded IWF "because it seemed to me that feminist groups by and large spoke to a very radicalized minority."[13] And, showing that it thinks of itself as speaking to and for a majority of women, IWF declares: "Who represents the *real* interests of American women? The IWF does, and here's how."[14]

CWA offers analogous reasoning about its representation of women. Although the organization clearly talks about being composed of and speaking for "Christian"[15] women, it also frequently asserts that it is "mainstream."[16] From the point of view of CWA, most Americans favor Judeo-Christian beliefs, and thus most women would (or should) accept CWA's moral and religious views. Those women who do not are considered to be, de facto, a fringe group in terms of their values and interests. Indeed, in speaking of which women CWA appeals to, group founder LaHaye claims: "the *vast majority* of women, thank God, want to raise children with integrity and strong character" in ways that CWA proposes it should be done.[17] Later in her book, LaHaye suggests that feminists who speak of representing women are disingenuous: "We cannot and must not accept their overblown claims about what a woman should be. Today's feminists are not honest about their beliefs or claims."[18]

As conservative organizations formed to challenge feminism, dismissing their opponents while making representative claims of their own is critical. It enables CWA and IWF to offer themselves as alternative options for women who seek advocates for their causes. In this way, they situate themselves as institutions that can represent women's interests. And, as women's organizations, they are not only able to fight feminists on their terms, but they are better suited than male-led conservative organizations to appeal to other conservative women who identify with CWA and IWF leadership. For them, merely being women's organizations has symbolic importance that increases their potential for influence. As I will show in the next sections, the organizations also stress the importance of placing women in leadership positions to make representative claims in the media and to policymakers.

A MEDIA VOICE FOR WOMEN

Mass media are critical outlets for interest groups because they assist organizations in their efforts to reach members, potential participants, and policymakers. Media also help to produce cultural images and rhetorical shifts in political issues, enabling activists to shape public opinion, influence policy outcomes, and construct ideas about their groups and social movements. Given the important role of media, advocates of all political stripes seek access and attempt to influence journalists and reporters. But the media are also favorite targets of disdain for many conservatives, who claim that liberals have a strong hold on the institution.[19] Consistent with its allies, CWA and IWF contend that conservative women's organizations are either dismissed by the media and/or portrayed as "crazy wing nut right wingers."[20] In response, since the mid-1908s, conservatives have built a solid network of radio- and television-based talk shows and other programming that simultaneously criticize the media and garner substantial publicity for conservative leaders, ideas, and values.

Contrary to their negative proclamations about press coverage, CWA and IWF have been relatively successful in obtaining media access, promoting what they consider to be "balanced" reporting and giving conservative leaders star power. One media watch group found that, in one year, "the *New York Times* published six opinion pieces by IWF leaders, the *Wall Street Journal* published five, the *Washington Post* three.... [D]uring the same period those same papers chose to publish no commentary on any subject by anyone from NOW...or the Feminist Majority Foundation."[21] In addition, a study of major newspapers demonstrated that print coverage of feminist organizations declined between 2002 and 2004, while attention to conservative women's groups increased.[22] An important component of their efforts to attract this attention is to interact with the media as women to challenge feminist organizations and the representation of women's identities and interests. For example, Anita Blair says this of IWF's founding as a women's organization:

> I think it was a reaction to particularly the media surrounding the Clarence Thomas/Anita Hill [situation] and the Year of the Woman. At that time you couldn't pick up a newspaper or listen to a radio or television program without hearing women think this or women think that. And invariably, it was a left-wing women's perspective. And most of us...felt that it was not at all a woman's perspective, because we were women and we had a different take on these things.[23]

Due in part to this perceived bias in the media, one of IWF's first projects was to publish a *Media Directory of Women Experts* that listed 300 "knowledgeable women who can provide *balanced* commentary on timely subjects ranging from 'Aviation' to 'Workplace Issues.'" IWF board member Wendy Gramm articulates why the organization felt the need to produce this type of publication:

> I always think it's great to have women as spokesmen [*sic*].... Even though we believe that we are not crazy about having hyphenated Americans.... But on the other hand we have found that for our organization that it has been helpful to have a woman going up there and saying something about this issue or that.... people may be more receptive if they hear it from a woman.[24]

Gramm, herself a "hyphenated American" (Asian American), sharply illustrates the tension felt by IWF because of its decision to strategically invoke gender identity. As her comments illustrate, since attributions based on gender and/or race conflict with its economic conservative ideology, the organization's leaders profess discomfort with making identity-based claims. In a move that seems contradictory, but which highlights the complexity of negotiating among its competing influences and goals, IWF does invoke gender identity by making claims as women in the media. It considers the presence of women on television and in print essential to its ability to succeed, and sends daily e-mails to its subscribers detailing where and when its leaders will be on television and/or the radio. There is some evidence that this push for airing the views of conservative women has garnered attention and positive media support for IWF and other conservative organizations.[25]

For its part, to attract more media attention, CWA has created a heightened public role for its president. Several staff told me that CWA decided to move its president into the role of spokesperson to get a woman's face in the media to represent them. "We are trying hard now with Carmen...to present that to the media, because we are not getting the media coverage that NOW gets. And we've got to stop that. We have 500,000 members, NOW has 60–70,000 and they get all the attention," bemoans CWA board member Jan Roberto.[26] Additionally, CWA's Rosaline Bush notes, "We feel that women need spokesmen. We do not believe that NOW speaks for us."[27] These organizations place a high premium on having women speak for them and on letting their members know that media have called upon conservative women to speak publicly about their work. An examination of CWA's "Media Center" and "Expert" Web site pages reveals, for example, clips of its female leaders' appearances, but there is little attention paid to the men who have spoken on its behalf.[28]

CWA and IWF position women front and center in public speaking roles to get coverage, gain legitimacy, and construct the conservative movement as diverse in terms of gender. Their efforts are not lost on the media either: cable news and political talk shows regularly feature conservative women as commentators. These include such major news outlets as NBC, C-SPAN, CNN, Court TV, Fox News, print newspapers, and radio talk shows.

WOMEN AS POLICY ACTIVISTS

Like the media, policymaking entities are important targets for CWA and IWF, as they are institutions through which women's identities and interests get constructed, defined, and addressed by laws. It is more difficult for conservatives to be attacked as "antiwoman" if women are making the political claims. CWA and IWF also alter the meaning of conservative issues by constructing them specifically in terms of women's interests. The organizations are well aware of the relevance of gender identity in this context and recognize the power they have when their female staff or members interact with lawmakers and the public. For example, when asked by a *Washington Post* reporter why "antifeminists" should form a women's organization, IWF's executive director, Barbara Ledeen, said: "You can't have white guys saying you don't need affirmative action. We feel we have credibility to say 'not all women think the way you may expect.'"[29] And, in discussing the impact of women lobbying against abortion, a CWA board member stated similarly: "Whereas if the answer is coming from a woman, it is likely to carry more credibility...coming from the mouth of a woman it would carry more weight."[30]

The value of "strategic essentialism" in this case is illuminated by CWA's former lobbyist, who argued that because men feel that they will be attacked by feminists and perhaps by the "liberal" media, women make better spokespeople on conservative issues:

> Sometimes it takes women to stand up and stomp their feet and say enough.... The Equal Rights Amendment was a perfect opportunity for that to happen; because that was so much perceived as a woman's fight and a woman's battle. Men were so scared to speak out, they still are.... But we are able to walk into a [congressional] office and say we represent 500,000 women in this country. That rings a bell.[31]

Like many interest groups with grassroots members, the ability to reference a large constituency to policymakers gives it political clout. To that end, CWA also hosts an annual "REAL Women Lobbying

Day" to gather women in DC to lobby members of Congress against legalized abortion. Kenda Bartlett, a CWA staff member, notes the power of having these women convene: "When our lobbyists go to Washington, DC, or our volunteers go [to Capitol Hill], and they say they represent the largest women's public policy organization in the United States, that has clout."[32]

Given the overblown stereotype of feminist women as man-haters, it benefits feminist organizations to get public and legislative support from men for their policy concerns. CWA and IWF, however, rely on just the opposite approach in order to be taken seriously as delegates for women. For these conservative women's organizations, who advocate for policies that many feminists and liberals see as antiwoman, having women speak should give them broader appeal among conservative constituencies and allies, policymakers and the public. As conservative organizations claiming to represent women, this can be a viable political strategy that enables CWA and IWF to take on feminists in the policymaking arena. The organizations' disregard for the paradox of such a tactic is intentional. Indeed, CWA and IWF know that they have been and will continue to be criticized for doing what they chastise feminists for doing. Nonetheless, they consider their actions to be politically necessary and thus bank on the likelihood that such behavior will not damage their credibility. This risky conduct is probably a wise investment: much of the criticism for their actions comes from feminists themselves. Unfavorable judgments from mainstream media, other conservatives, and the general public are notably absent. As for the media in these cases, their lack of negativity may be the result of journalists' responding to the criticisms, accurate or not, that they have been too liberal and/or biased against those involved with right-wing politics.

Organizing as women and having women speak for them are particular forms of strategic essentialism that both organizations have adopted. But what about stressing the relationship between identity and interests? Do CWA and IWF believe or further the idea that women really have such distinct interests from men that they require women deliberating and making policy decisions in organizations run by and for women? The answers to these questions reveal differences between the two organizations and can be attributed to the ideological cleavages between them. The socially conservative CWA is generally more comfortable, eager, and willing than IWF to emphasize biological differences between women and men. They also more readily claim that these differences translate into women having distinct interests from men. The more libertarian IWF produces mixed messages on the subject. In addressing why it formed into a women's organization, IWF argues that women's differences from each other are more important than those between women and men. However, as I will show in Chapter Five, on issues like mothering and child care, IWF is quick to argue that women make better primary caretakers than do men, in part because of their natures. In that case, IWF posits views consistent with those of CWA, exposing moments of fluidity between social and economic conservatives, but also exhibiting the fact that IWF is conflicted on the relative salience of gender differences to its political activism.

A DISTINCT WOMEN'S PERSPECTIVE?

Since both organizations consider the differences between men and women to be natural, one would expect organizational beliefs that reflect these values, with claims that women's organizations are necessary because women have distinct needs and viewpoints from men. This perspective, for example, has motivated some women to engage in political activism because of what they consider to be their unique experiences and interests as mothers.[33] That is, they believe that interests follow identity. While this generally holds true for CWA, as noted, IWF is more circumspect in making such a pronouncement. Why this divergence?

As I outlined in chapter 1, CWA and IWF do represent different constituencies. CWA's base is composed mostly of social conservatives who favor "traditional" gender roles. IWF's looser network of associates is activated by economically conservative views that stress individualism over collective action and identity. The need to appeal to and mobilize their differing conservative constituencies mediates the extent to which these organizations stress the correlation between gender identity and women's interests—particularly as this correlation relates to the reasons they formed women's organizations and to their ability to achieve political success. CWA, for example, believes that women's unique perspectives qualify them to make group-based political claims. One CWA staffer sums it up this way: "I think that the true woman, mother, family member's voice, needs to be heard more than it is....We definitely view the family as why we're doing what we're doing, but with the woman's vantage point."[34] Similarly, Carmen Pate, who was the president of CWA at the time of our interview, notes how the organization seeks to speak for women:

With every issue, we can bring in why it should be of concern to women, and that is what we try to do: why mom should be concerned, why wives should be concerned, why you should be concerned about your daughters. That is the connection that we try to make. How will this impact women long term?[35]

CWA was founded to oppose the Equal Rights Amendment and to fight other policies that it believes disrupt traditional gender roles and norms. Its leaders have been criticized for engaging in "professional" careers, but it justifies this discrepancy when it makes claims to be helping other women to realize their potential as wives and mothers. Indeed, for the activists associated with this religious conservative group, their work is considered to be a calling or mission. And strategically, for CWA, its efforts are considered to be absolutely necessary: what better way for women to be mobilized into conservative political causes than to follow other conservative women? Its founder, Beverly LaHaye, got to the heart of this sentiment when she wrote: "We women need heroines. We want to see living examples of Christian women who stand against the immoral, godless, feminist teaching."[36]

Both organizations believe that having women speak for them gives them credibility to represent women and to challenge feminists. It is entirely different, however, to say that women's messages are different from men's because of biology and familial and social roles. While each organization favors a messenger who is female, only CWA claims that its identity as a women's organization also hinges on women's differences from men. IWF does not dispute that women are different from men, but it does not consider that to be the basis for its founding. Instead, it argues that only the differences among women, not between women and men, warranted its forming into a women's organization. As IWF's Anita Blair told me: "[W]e just simply wanted to show, to coin a phrase, that gender is not determinism. You know, your sex does not dictate your political views. So the IWF in particular wanted to present another voice. We wanted to be a voice for women who had different views."[37]

Blair's comments sharply illustrate how the use of gender as a primary organizing principle creates tensions for the organization. In the same breath, she denounces the relationship between gender identity and interests while explaining why her organization emphasizes this connection when advocating for policy goals. In discussing this paradoxical manifestation of identity politics, another IWF associate notes this about the organization's leaders:

[T]hey come from a philosophical background that leads them to believe that they are interested in what the argument is, not who the deliverer of the argument is. So...the challenge was finding people to actually run the organization, and in a sense *limit* themselves.[38]

Because of IWF's strong belief in individualism and distaste for identity politics, it has to justify its being a women's organization. As noted, it does so in highly strategic terms, conceding to feminists the relative value of acting as women. IWF, however, also considers gender-based identity activism to be "limiting" in that it has the potential to exclude men and economic conservative women who do not see their interests as being collectively defined and determined.

For IWF, being a women's organization and positioning women in leadership roles is a strategy, but the relationship between identity and interests is continuously qualified while simultaneously being invoked. Such contradictory behavior may give opponents cause to dismiss the work of the organization, but it is a price that IWF is willing to pay to be taken seriously as the antidote to feminist organizational actions.

WHEN CONSERVATIVE IDEOLOGY TRUMPS GENDER

There are times when both CWA and IWF readily repudiate the significance of gender identity. Given findings that women in elected office prioritize women's interests,[39] one might expect that CWA and IWF would want to increase the number of women in political office to heighten attention to women's issues. Neither organization, however, devotes resources to increasing the number of women in public office.

Based on IWF's criticism of the relationship between identity and interests in other contexts, its views about women in public office are not that surprising. In fact, the organization is close to hostile on the subject. Writing for IWF's *Women's Quarterly*, national advisory board member Kate O'Beirne had this to say about Republican leaders' consideration of putting Elizabeth Dole on a presidential ticket:

They [Republican Party leaders] hope to appeal to women voters by engaging in bean-counting identity politics that is now outdated but perfectly suits Elizabeth Dole. Indeed, Mrs. Dole is the figurehead for a generation of Republican women who dominate the party structure, but whose dearly held feminist convictions often conflict with its conservative constituency and the politics of younger Republican women.[40]

O'Beirne's views closely match the sentiments of the IWF leaders interviewed for this book. IWF contends that, aside from the few feminist elites in both parties, most women are not interested in identity politics when it comes to who is representing them in the White House, the Congress, or their statehouses. Leaders suggest that the organization would prefer to put its efforts into working with any elected official willing to support its agenda.

CWA also denies that women elected officials would be more likely than men to bring different policy concerns to a legislative body's agenda. Contradicting its tenet that interests and gender are linked, it argues for supporting candidates and elected officials based on issues, not identity. There are several possible explanations for this inconsistent position.

First, the push to increase the number of women in public office appears to be too similar to affirmative action—a policy that CWA and many other conservative organizations oppose.[41] While proponents of affirmative action believe that it helps to mitigate discrimination based on (perceived) gender and racial differences, most conservatives do not. Many are outspoken critics who actively work to overturn affirmative action policies. Here, for example, CWA's Seriah Rein rejects the tactic of electing more women to public office by connecting the process to affirmative action:

> I don't think you need to have cancer to be able to articulate how to prevent it and how to deal with it and how to treat it. I don't believe in quotas period. I know some men who can more effectively express the concerns of women than a lot of women I know....I don't think you should have a certain percentage of women for the sake of having women, I think that is the big disservice we did with blacks in affirmative action....I feel the same way about women being represented in Congress.[42]

A second reason for CWA's eschewing the strategy of getting more women into public office is that empirical studies suggest that women elected officials tend to be more liberal than their male counterparts within the same party.[43] Given these findings, CWA may not be in any hurry to call for the election of more women lawmakers, as it is likely aware that the majority of women who win elective office are more liberal than the women whom the organization represents. Additionally, there are already many men in public office who support its policy agendas.

Although CWA does not embrace the idea of increasing the number of women in office, its former lobbyist, Laurel MacLeod, acknowledges that some women elected officials may have more credibility on its issues than do men. Thus, CWA may seek out like-minded women legislators to speak on behalf of its issues at key times during a political contest. As MacLeod confides: "If you had more women in Congress like Linda Smith and Helen Chenoweth, who are prolife and are willing to go down and speak out, and on some issues really give courage to the men, I would see that as an enormous and very positive change."[44] In light of MacLeod's comments, it might be unwise for these organizations to dismiss the push for more women in political office. Research indicates that 60% of women candidates run as Democrats, suggesting a party gap among women who seek political office.[45] In addition, the literature on the impact of women in public office does find that a range of women bring "women's traditional areas of concern"[46] to the policymaking process.[47] Since the particulars of these traditional areas of concern are often broad enough to encompass conservative women's concerns, both feminist and conservative women have the potential to shake things up once in office. Certainly, as this book shows, conservative women care about women's issues as much as feminist and liberal women do. They just construct them in different ways. Thus, conservative women's organizations might benefit from conservative women's election to office. That they have chosen not to actively encourage and support women's moving into elected public leadership positions suggests the need as women's organizations to appeal to and mobilize their conservative allies, at the risk of allowing feminists to maintain a stronghold on this strategy. In addition, since scholars have also found that elected women cite the support of women's organizations as a resource,[48] efforts by CWA and IWF to bolster the number of conservative women in office could pay off for them in terms of having their policy goals promoted in legislative bodies. The success of groups like the Susan B. Anthony List, a political action committee that raises funds for antiabortion female candidates, which has grown exponentially since the mid-1990s,[49] exemplifies the power that conservatives can have when they choose to help further the careers of women candidates and politicians.

CONCLUSIONS

Both organizations consider gender identity to be an organizational resource and thus recognize some value in strategic essentialism. In this chapter, I have suggested that having to negotiate between conservative ideology and the need to make broad claims on behalf of women helps to determine the form in which and the extent to which gender identity is actually invoked. In other words, as others have shown in studies about women seeking political standing, context matters.[50] In this case, both groups want to attenuate the association of women's advocacy with feminism, but it is clear that their differing ideological commitments factor into how problems are defined and who articulates concerns to the public. CWA holds a more essentialist view of women's identities and interests and promotes these beliefs not only by positioning women in key leadership positions, but by (mostly) advocating for a women's perspective that is distinct from men's. In so doing, it signifies women as different from men and advances its views about gender roles. Consistent, then, with its socially conservative ideology and desire to contest feminist representational claims, CWA positions itself as an organization that speaks to and works to construct the "true" nature of women's interests.

IWF is more self-consciously essentialist in its deployment of the category "women," and mostly invokes gender identity to raise the question of *which* women's interests are getting represented. In its case, engagement with identity politics is a reactive gesture, one meant to counter feminist political actions. This strategy emanates from the need to risk essentialism in order to achieve the political goals of showing that women can be conservative and proving that feminists are wrong in their interpretations of women's interests.

It is critical that we understand the power these organizations can have because they have chosen these strategies. Diana Fuss argues that political identities do not precede politics, but are derivative of them.[51] That conservative women disrupt feminist political interventions confirms what critics say about the necessity of recognizing how interests are neither fixed nor predetermined, but are products of the interactions among advocates, policymakers, and the public. For example, what we consider to be "women's" interests and experiences are really constituted when a group called "women" makes claims about itself. For feminists, identity politics as initiated by conservative women presents a twofold challenge. Most immediate are the competing claims about desired policy outcomes, which shape debates and laws. A second, although no less significant, concern is that when groups like CWA and IWF make collective claims, they force feminists to concede that identity politics has significant limits. As noted, some have argued for reconceptualizing identity politics,[52] but rarely do these discussions recognize the deep ideological differences among women. Instead, conservative women are located outside the group "women" that most feminists reference, supporting Butler's contention about the exclusionary nature of identity politics.

As I will show in the following chapters, CWA and IWF have capitalized on this consequence, arguing that feminists are elitist, out of touch, or merely inattentive to the range of concerns that women articulate. Although they have not always been successful in completely undermining feminist advocacy, they have had key moments when their efforts have been rewarded.

Chapter 4

ARE WOMEN VICTIMS?
Framing Violence against Women

Advocacy concerning violence against women policies comes from both feminist and conservative women. But until recently, feminist organizations have shaped the terrain on this issue, and thus CWA and IWF are playing on a field where feminists have been active for some time. Through the efforts of national and local feminist organizations, violence against women is taken much more seriously by policymakers and the public now than it was when the second wave of the feminist movement was gaining momentum. For example, in 1970, there were no shelters for battered women in the United States. Now, over 2,000 exist across the country, according to the National Coalition against Domestic Violence.[1] True, many lawmakers have required and continue to need consistent prodding, but as evidenced by the historic passage of the federal Violence Against Women Act (VAWA) in 1994,[2] a good number of them have been receptive.

The success of feminists in defining the problem of violence against women is not lost on CWA and IWF. As organizations seeking to be taken seriously as advocates for women, it is incumbent upon them to respond to the efforts and successes of the feminist movement. They must face the reality that feminists have set the agenda on violence against women, an issue that feminists contend starkly reveals ideas about women's status within society. Consistent with the "personal is political" theme of the second wave feminist movement, activists have headed down the long and difficult road of getting people to take seriously sexual assault, harassment, and battering against women and their children. This includes the recognition that "changing the conditions that foster violence requires changing cultural perspectives and priorities."[3] In other words, feminists have argued and continue to contend that violence is not just about individual behavior, but about the social and gendered meanings of aggression and how these play out in relationships between men and women. So where do conservative women fit into these debates? How do they legitimate themselves as representatives of women's interests when it comes to explaining and ameliorating political and social conditions that enable acts of violence against women? If they oppose feminists, they risk being perceived as callous. If they side with feminists, their conservative allies may shun them. In addition, this is not merely a political contest over who can claim the right to know what women's interests are in the case of violence against women. Like all policy battles, it is about the struggle for scarce resources, public support, lawmakers' attention, and policy outcomes.

In this chapter, I will demonstrate how CWA and IWF invoke a complex set of arguments to articulate their positions on violence against women and to mediate among the challenges they face as conservative and women's organizations. Their narratives reflect a desire to transform the meaning of violence against women while attending to the political context in which this issue has become prominent. While tackling the problem of violence against women involves myriad goals and policies, CWA and IWF address the issue in fairly narrow terms. For CWA, the topic surfaces through the organization's work in opposing pornography. That is, it charges that pornography can cause men to inflict physical and emotional harm on women. As I will discuss, addressing the issue of violence against women through pornography enables CWA to negotiate well between feminist influences and conservative goals and constituencies. For IWF, violence against women is raised when it debates the value of VAWA and when it advocates for changes in sexual harassment laws. Its stance on these particular issues allows IWF to advocate for women while promoting economic conservative ideas about government function and size. That IWF does not take a stance on pornography is also likely a function of these ideas, as IWF prefers limited regulation of social and economic interactions.

When it comes to addressing violence against women, the organizations deviate from one another in terms of how they frame feminist objectives. CWA argues that women are victims—not of feminists, but of male violence and corrupted cultural norms. While it occasionally indicts feminism for helping to create a climate where pornography is widely available and accepted, it mostly employs arguments similar to those of feminists—about women's integrity and safety—and bridges them with social conservative arguments about morality and "traditional" family values. IWF asserts that feminists have grossly exaggerated and distorted the problem of violence against women by using false statistics to promote their beliefs and boost their resources. It does go on the record to say that domestic violence is a serious problem,[4] but it emphatically chastises feminists for cultivating a climate where women are encouraged to feel like victims, to scapegoat men, and to require government intervention to remedy their problems. With regard to the issue of violence against women, we also see variations between CWA and IWF in terms of their views about the role of state involvement in social programs. CWA is amenable to federal intervention when it considers such actions to be supportive in the promotion of social conservative values. Its advocacy for a constitutional amendment advancing prayer in schools is an example of this perspective. As an economic conservative organization that favors localizing and privatizing social services, IWF fervently challenges efforts to federalize the distribution of funds for services like shelters and antiviolence programs. These ideological differences come through when analyzing CWA's and IWF's activism around violence against women issues.

Although they are not alike in their assessments of women's interests in this case, they have in common the use of the three frames detailed in Chapter One: antifeminist, women's interests, and social/economic conservative. By juxtaposing these narratives, CWA and IWF engage in adaptive framing strategies that help to position them as organizational advocates responding to violence against women. Although their rhetoric results in the articulation of divergent policy goals, they share the desire to construct themselves as representatives of women and to present women-friendly interpretations of conservative issues.

CWA AND PORNOGRAPHY: SEEING WOMEN AS VICTIMS

For CWA, opposing pornography is one of its key policy priorities and the issue through which it expresses its concerns about violence against women. The organization supports strict regulation of the industry and urges pornography "addicts," as it calls them, to seek counseling through church-based programs. Consistent with its struggle to instill conservative morals and keep traditional heterosexual families intact, CWA contends that pornography persuades men to demean their wives, to ruin their marriages, and to engage in illicit sexual behaviors. Its disdain for pornography, a position consistent with the organization's social conservative views on sexuality and marriage, is also frequently framed in terms of messages about women's empowerment and freedom from violence. While it occasionally blames feminists for helping to promote sexual freedom and promiscuity, it simultaneously transforms its social conservative views to be more consistent with feminist rhetoric about the potential effects of pornography.

Feminism and the Degradation of Cultural Values

Unlike with its other issues, CWA is less specifically and forcefully anti-feminist in dealing with pornography. In fact, its framing of pornography in terms of women's interests is nearly identical to the protestations made by feminists who oppose pornography. Feminist activism with regard to pornography has a different history than feminist advocacy around other domestic violence issues. That is, not all feminists oppose pornography. Some argue that restrictions on pornography violate the First Amendment right to free speech and that this form of censorship is dangerous, especially to women, who typically have little say in what gets banned.[5] Additionally, some support the personal rights of women to engage in the industry and to enjoy pornography themselves.[6] This chapter is not meant to deny or endorse the legitimacy of these arguments. However, CWA opposes pornography and frequently asserts itself on grounds akin to those of antipornography feminists, who have tried to pass laws restricting the production and distribution of pornography. Of late, feminist organizations have devoted very little attention to the issue of pornography, giving conservative groups like CWA the opportunity to lead the challenges against it. In this sense, CWA is not necessarily trying to take the issue away from feminists, but is instead staking out a particular place among conservatives as an organization devoted to addressing the social consequences of pornography and its effects on women. Given that 43% of American women favor laws forbidding the distribution of pornography to anyone, their efforts are not out of line with a significant portion of the female public.[7]

The "feminists" referenced in this section are those who oppose pornography. Two of the most vocal and well known of these opponents are Catharine MacKinnon and Andrea Dworkin. Neither is on the staff of the feminist organizations most cited by CWA and IWF: MacKinnon is a feminist legal scholar and professor of law, and the late Dworkin was a well-known feminist activist and author. Nonetheless, both have helped to bring significant attention to what they consider to be the problems with pornography. Generally, they argue that pornography should be recognized as a violation of women's civil rights, as a form of sex discrimination, and as a symptom and cause of violence against women.[8] MacKinnon urges that, legally, pornography should be considered more than "speech" and contends that "protecting pornography means protecting sexual abuse *as* speech."[9] Although CWA would not agree with MacKinnon on other issues,[10] it does make analogous claims about pornography. To be clear, CWA mostly limits its discussion about pornography to materials that project adult heterosexual activity. It does, at times, also reference pornography that involves children to use that material as evidence in its debates against pedophilia.

In terms of its discussions about feminism and pornography, CWA alleges that feminists are self-serving, but its disdain for feminism factors little into its analysis of the problems with pornography. Feminism, however, is blamed in part for the debasement of public morality and the ascent of the sexual revolution—two factors that CWA cites for increasing pornography's accessibility, availability, and popularity. Chronicling a shift in social norms and values, one CWA writer argues:

> Feminists convinced many women they could have it all—and Super Mom was born. She cleaned, cooked, cuddled babies, coddled her husband—and commuted to the office. The result? Exhausted women who resented husband and family; unfulfilled women leaving home to "find themselves"; and men who had been stripped of their role as head of the family. No-fault divorce laws made it easy for couples to "start over"—again and again. A "do your own thing" mentality left children low on the list of parental priorities.... And the ongoing battle between the sexes forced all sorts of perversions out of the closet and into the mainstream.[11]

According to this narrative, feminism has helped to produce the cultural dynamics that allow pornography to exist. That is, feminists are held accountable for men being unfulfilled since they encourage women to seek personal satisfaction, sometimes at the expense of their marriages and families. CWA also feels that women's self-centered behavior could lead to the destruction of the traditional family—an institution that it considers to be the bedrock of a stable society.

Despite its criticisms of feminists, CWA has suggested that it could possibly work together with them to combat the pornography industry. Of this potential collaboration with feminist organizations, Kathy Arrington, a former Bible study teacher, CWA state leader, and one-time director of CWA's national board, told me: "sometimes we agree on certain things, but we don't seem to work together on those....I would think issues in the area of pornography [are] an example, because it certainly breaks down the family and is harmful to women."[12]

She adds, however, that she does not think feminists would want to work with CWA because of other, major ideological differences. Given that CWA also grounds its claims against pornography in terms of its opposition to gay rights and to sex outside of marriage, Arrington is likely to be accurate. Historically, neither feminists nor conservative women have made efforts to cooperate, even if they might find common ground on some issues. Although political partners sometimes make for strange bedfellows, neither feminist nor conservative women's national interest groups have felt comfortable pooling their efforts and resources on most national policy efforts. There has been too much tension and antagonism between them over the years to allow for much trust or sisterhood.

Notwithstanding some criticism of feminists on the issue of violence against women, CWA frames much of its opposition to pornography in terms of women's interests. And, as I show in the following analysis, CWA's critiques of pornography are often hard to distinguish from those of its feminist counterparts.

Women as Victims of Pornography

CWA holds regular "Victims of Pornography Month" briefings on Capitol Hill, where it urges members of Congress to heed that pornography is not a "victimless crime" but one that affects "women and children whose bodies are used like disposable items."[13] The topic is one of seven core issues on CWA's agenda and has been a central focus of the organization since the 1990s. Pornography is cited as being harmful to men, who can become addicted to it, but the consequences of this dependency are frequently evaluated in terms of its effects on women. Aside from the expected discussion of familial discord, pornography is also said to give men the negative impression that "all women are available for their pleasure as mere sex objects."[14] A judge who ruled in favor of allowing pornography on military bases was chastised for abandoning "the interests of women and children,"[15] while Hugh Hefner, founder of *Playboy* magazine, is described as the "man who preached hatred against women."[16]

According to CWA, pornography is directly correlated with incidences of violence against women. It claims that men's exposure to pornography can have devastating effects on women because men can become desensitized to rape and battering and start to consider these behaviors to be normal. This is due in part to the fact that some pornography portrays women enjoying violent treatment. In an article published in CWA's glossy membership magazine, *Family Voice*, the organization suggests a direct correlation between pornography and violence against women by noting that "86 percent of all rapists admit to using pornography regularly."[17] In another piece documenting the addictive nature of pornography, CWA offers this dire observation:

> Serial killer Ted Bundy attributed his criminal record to the *Playboy* magazines he collected in the 1950s as a 12-year-old boy. They juxtaposed sex and violence and fostered an unnatural desire to kill women for sexual pleasure. In his last interview, he warned about the danger today's pornography poses to society. "What scares and appalls me ... is when I see what's on cable TV, some of the movies and some of the violence in the movies that comes into homes today, with stuff that they wouldn't show in X-rated adult theaters [30] years ago," Bundy said. "[What will happen] as it gets into the home of children who may be unattended or unaware that they may be a Ted Bundy[?]"[18]

These strongly worded statements from CWA exemplify its belief that pornography should be considered violence against women. Like many antiporn feminists, CWA cautions that pornography's use and availability hurt women by creating a cultural climate in which women are objectified and not taken seriously by the judicial system in cases where they press charges against sexual assailants and rapists. It also fears that pornography leads to men mistreating their wives, having affairs, and/or abandoning their marriages. It publishes stories detailing the experiences of women whose husbands are "hooked" on pornography and warns women that "psychologists say addiction to porn warps a man's relationship with women, producing more divorce and sexual abuse in America."[19]

Its condemnation of pornography reveals how CWA offers arguments that feminists would recognize. It urges women to prioritize their own interests and chastises men for inflicting pain on their spouses. For example, the organization reminds its woman reader that she "should never stay in a marriage in which her husband sexually or physically abuses her."[20] CWA supports and counsels women to protect themselves and encourages clergy to help women too. In speaking about the harm posed to women, CWA projects an image of conservatism that is commensurate with feminist interpretations of how to care for women in these situations.

In addition to trying to stop men from consuming pornography, CWA also advocates for strict regulation of the pornography industry. It holds that the people involved in promoting pornography work against the interests of women and children. Here, it echoes criticisms made public by one-time porn star Linda Lovelace,[21] that the industry not only exploits women through its cultural messages, but also victimizes and cheats those who work in the business. Thus, it encourages lawmakers to take on pornographers by suggesting criminal intent on the part of the industry:

> Porn producers would be the first to say that pornography is not a crime—and it has no victims. They claim that porn actors—performing everything from sadistic sex to bestiality—are having the times of their lives. But women and children who have been forced to engage in these productions tell a different story....It should be evident to everyone that coercion—used to humiliate, silence and blackmail women and children—is the backbone of the pornography industry.[22]

Since eliminating or regulating pornography is difficult (much of it is protected as free speech under the First Amendment of the U.S. Constitution), CWA has turned its policy efforts toward working to get restrictions placed on access to pornography on the Internet. In this case, it calls for service providers and the boards of libraries and schools to limit what can be viewed by minors, and it filed an amicus brief in a case before the U.S. Supreme Court to that effect.[23] It also lobbies aggressively for stricter FCC controls over the content of broadcast television and radio programs.

While CWA would no doubt prefer that pornography be outlawed, advocating this position would take the organization nowhere. Thus, its efforts to represent women's interests in this case are directed at changing cultural norms and values and engaging in debates over how new technologies might be regulated. For the latter, CWA also articulates its concerns in terms of children's interests, a population that tends to elicit more sympathy than women do.

With regard to its overall policy agenda, CWA's framing of issues as women's interests involves a complex interplay between ideology and strategy. That is, CWA does indeed believe that women are at risk from pornography. In this sense, its frames emanate from the belief systems of the women who lead the organization. But, as an organization vying with feminists over who legitimately represents women, CWA also recognizes the value of making representative claims in the name of women. Thus, the framing of policy goals in terms of women's interests reflects its conservative ideology about gendered norms but also stems from a desire to establish credibility as a women's organization. In this latter sense, it is a strategic action. As such, its women's interests frames transform social conservative arguments into those that may resonate with women who are concerned about pornography's outcomes but who otherwise have made few connections to social conservative organizations or arguments. As noted, a majority of women, from a range of backgrounds, cite reducing domestic violence and sexual assault as the top priority for a women's movement.[24] By linking pornography to violence against women, CWA ably taps into women's concerns.

CWA not only indicts the industry for exploiting women, but also blames pornography for cultivating a cultural climate ripe with social degradation and perversion. Through this social conservative frame, it speaks directly to its base, keeping its ties to supporters as it works to expand its reach. In the following section, I elaborate on CWA's invocation of frames in these cases.

Social Conservative Arguments

For CWA, fighting pornography means engaging in an ideological battle and tackling beliefs that have disrupted the purity of American values. This means seeing pornography as both a symptom and a cause of unchecked sexuality and "nontraditional" relationships. CWA implores the federal government to "return the stigma to porn."[25] And a CWA lobbyist told me that the best way to address the issue of pornography is to attack it on a cultural level:

> I think the best way to deal with [pornography] is the way we've dealt with smoking. Social sanctions and enforce the laws. And accountability for harm. The pornography industry as an institution does a lot of harm to a lot of people. If they could be held accountable for the harm they did, it wouldn't be quite as lucrative.... That person needs to get sued. Think about the harm it does to the people whose images are used, I mean it's basically prostitutes. Prostitution and pornography and drug addiction are all three facets of the same thing—slavery.[26]

These strong words reflect the organization's social conservative status. Its leaders seek to change values and to influence moral behavior through both education and policymaking endeavors. Generally, since CWA tries to appeal to a broad scope of women and men, it does not always reference its conservative religious beliefs. But, as a social conservative organization whose membership consists primarily of conservative evangelicals, it is necessary for CWA to use language reflective of its ideological roots. For instance, it bemoans the lack of attention to the issue by church leaders and denounces more liberal denominations for failing to consider that there may be a relationship between pornography and homosexuality. It may alienate some women to hear arguments couched in religious terms, but CWA's mission and membership are rooted in conservative religious traditions. References to its theology, then, help to shore up its loyal constituency.

Its narratives about adult pornography are also tied into the organization's opposition to homosexuality, extramarital sex, and child pornography. For example, CWA argues that some pornography can lead to pedophilia and cause men to assault young boys. For CWA, pornography threatens the stability of the heterosexual relationship—the cornerstone of a good family, according to CWA. The organization also maintains that exposure to pornography damages a man's sense of responsibility and inscribes a warped sense of masculinity. It considers both of these outcomes to be harmful to women. As such, concerns about the interests of women are tied into the organization's social conservative values about family and gender roles, as exemplified by the following commentary in one of its publications:

> Before Hefner, real men scorned pornography. Real men had relationships with their wives. Even libertarian sex researchers concluded— much to their chagrin—that most men of the 1950s and 1960s actually "saved" themselves for marriage. They considered sex "too precious" to share with anyone but their wives. Premarital sex, they believed, was harmful. But *Playboy* made commitment a dirty word. The magazine counseled men to love 'em and leave 'em—fast. It featured cartoons sexualizing children and phony letters from women extolling bizarre sex practices. It belittled marriage and encouraged drug use.[27]

Coming from a women's organization, CWA's pronouncements about marriage and the need for men to commit to their wives may sound prudish, but they also sound less patronizing than conservative men projecting these thoughts. CWA's social conservative views about pornography are tied up with values that many feminists might find offensive, but coupled with its concerns about violence against women, it offers a more complicated and women-friendly assessment than conservative groups that focus solely on the "family values" or morality component of the problem.

Like IWF, CWA considers the eradication of violence against women to be a policy priority. For CWA, concerns about pornography stem from its social conservative views about sexuality and relationships, but reflect its desire to speak directly to the effects of this industry on women. In so doing, CWA establishes itself as a group that acts for women, all women, but in ways that may particularly appeal to its membership. Many of its arguments bear a strong likeness to those of feminists who oppose pornography, suggesting that its stance against pornography may be able to mobilize a broad range of women who care about the issue.

IWF AND VIOLENCE AGAINST WOMEN

What has become known as the battered women's movement started in the 1970s with local shelters and grew into programs that trained police and judicial personnel and provided financial and psychological services for victims. Feminists urged for stricter penalties for batterers and programs to help battered women and their children leave their abusive situations and start new lives. Advocates worked to publicize occurrences of violence against women and demanded that action be taken to help women who faced abuse at the hands of their intimate partners. Their efforts were rewarded by the passage of state and local laws, but many still felt that the federal government lacked a real commitment to addressing the problem.

In 1994, however, feminist advocates pushed the issue at the national level and worked with members of Congress and President Bill Clinton to pass VAWA. VAWA has since been reauthorized twice—in 2000 and again in 2005. This landmark legislation represents a strong commitment from policymakers to tackle the issues of domestic violence and rape. Despite being a rare bipartisan success at the national level, IWF opposes VAWA and many of its provisions. For example, it filed an amicus brief in *U.S. v. Morrison* to strike down a provision of VAWA that allowed women to file federal civil rights violations claims against abusers. The *Morrison* case was brought by Christy Brzonkala, a young woman who charged that two varsity football players assaulted her in a Virginia Tech college dorm in 1994. Ultimately, neither player was punished under university procedures, so Brzonkala sought relief in federal court, as VAWA laid out these federal civil rights remedies under the Interstate Commerce Clause and the Equal Protection Clause of the Fourteenth Amendment. The U.S. Supreme Court ruled that Congress lacks authority under the commerce clause to regulate conduct that is neither "interstate" nor "commerce," as the Court deemed was the case in *U.S. v. Morrison*. The Court also charged that claiming that her assault violated the Equal Protection Clause was invalid, because the Fourteenth Amendment prohibits only state action, that is, action by state governments, not private conduct. In so ruling, a majority of the justices overturned this provision of VAWA.

IWF's amicus brief position was congruent with the majority opinion in the U.S. Supreme Court case. Consistent with its economic conservative beliefs, IWF considered the civil rights provision to be an unreasonable extension of federal powers. According to IWF, at issue was whether or not the Constitution gives the federal government a "general police power" to regulate state activities. In addition, the organization suggested that requiring women to pursue federal rather than local remedies in such cases wastes their time and money. In later sections, I will discuss these arguments in more depth. Below, however, I elaborate on IWF's criticism of feminists with regard to VAWA—and its accusation that Congress was misled by feminist advocacy research about domestic violence. That is, IWF maintains that feminists exaggerated the extent and frequency of violence against women so that they could secure money to fund programs that promote liberal ideology.

Just the Facts, Feminists

A raison d'être for the IWF is to "correct" what it considers to be feminist myths about a variety of public policies, including violence against women. Feminists, according to IWF, lie about data, are opportunistic, construct men as the enemy, and cast women as helpless victims. Building on the controversial and well-publicized work of Christina Hoff Sommers,[28] IWF questions feminists' integrity and charges that domestic violence legislation is misleading because it is premised on and meant to advance feminist ideology.[29] To highlight what it sees as distortion and hyperbole on the part of feminists, IWF uses flippant, irreverent headlines, such as "Slap Your Spouse, Lose Your House"[30] and "Stop Beating Me, I've Got to Make a Phone Call,"[31] to frame its stories about domestic violence policies.

The organization contends that feminists consistently and convincingly use false statistics—with members of Congress, in the classroom, with the media—to the extent that they have become accepted and even widely held truths. For example, on the subject of VAWA, one IWF staff member remarks:

> [T]he feminist advocacy groups were able to create new bogus statistics faster than the experts were able to shoot the old ones down. And some of the untruths—like the fiction that wife-beating soars on Super Bowl Sunday—have become American myths as durable as the story of young George Washington chopping down the cherry tree.[32]

In her 1994 book, *Who Stole Feminism?*, Christina Hoff Sommers critiques feminists for claiming, without systematic empirical evidence, that incidences of domestic violence increase dramatically on Super Bowl Sunday. Hence IWF's reference above to that "fiction." Over the years, IWF has continued to publicize Sommers's argument, and in 2000 used this information in a legal contest over VAWA. IWF summarizes the claims it made in the amicus brief filed in *U.S. v. Morrison* by noting that VAWA was premised upon "deceitful data that appeared in the legislative history [of the bill]."[33] Aside from this case, it offers little evidence that feminist interpretations of data are widely held public "truths." Nonetheless, its framing of feminists as persuasive liars shows that the organization believes that feminists have set the agenda when it comes to violence against women. As such, IWF argues that feminists control public and political perceptions of women's interests and have thus shut down the ability of other women to make claims about these issues. To this conservative organization, feminists are a selfish, hegemonic group of actors seeking resources and recognition at the expense of most women. This belief is made evident in a press release issued by IWF about VAWA:

> Once again left-wing feminists can't seem to distinguish their own interests from the interests of real women who are victims of sexual assault. If Congress and the feminist activists who lobbied for VAWA really cared about protecting victims, they would emphasize local crime prevention, followed by strong support for local prosecution.[34]

This public declaration demonstrates how IWF mediates its antifeminist views through its economic conservative beliefs about the need for local government involvement in most social service programs, and it reflects the "tough on crime" philosophy generally espoused by conservatives. It also reaffirms IWF's support for conservative views that call for "federalist principles" that recognize the boundaries between state and national power.[35] Another example of this juxtaposition is articulated by IWF when it chastises feminists for encouraging women to sue the *federal* government for violence against women. Here, IWF charges that women's true interests take a backseat to feminist visions of justice. IWF founder Anita Blair sums up that opinion this way: "Had the Violence Against Women Act never been enacted, Ms. Brzonkala[36] could have had her day in a Virginia court long ago. Instead, her interests have been hijacked by opportunistic feminists and trial lawyers.... This federal law makes America safe for lawyers, not women."[37]

Such alleged hijacking by feminists also troubles IWF because it believes that, through VAWA and other government-funded violence prevention programs, feminists can use institutional power and resources to promote their values. Thus, IWF is not only critical of these policies because they are made at and can be enforced by the federal level of government, but also because these laws are made in consultation with feminists. As a result, claims IWF, VAWA not only "creates a symbiotic relationship between the federal government and the battered women's advocacy movement," but allows state domestic violence coalitions, which are allegedly guided by feminist ideology, to "play a vital role in the allocation of VAWA grants and in overseeing the implementation of VAWA-based programs and policies."[38]

In the case of violence against women, IWF also holds that feminists demean men because, according to the organization, VAWA lacks adequate support for programs that address violence against men. In these narratives, its antifeminism is loud and clear. It blames feminists for cultivating an environment where male bashing is acceptable and pervasive. To counteract feminist ideology, IWF calls for more attention to "female aggression"[39] and runs stories on researchers who claim they have been dismissed for exploring the role of women in provoking domestic violence situations.[40] IWF's sentiments are well summarized by a male supporter of the organization: "My sex needs to hire a press agent to offset the received wisdom that men can do no right and women can do no wrong."[41]

What is important to understand about IWF is that its antifeminist frames are not merely expressions of its values but serve important purposes. They provide women with both the rationale and language to contest feminist activism on grounds established by other women, not men. Promoting this sense of camaraderie may mobilize women—even those who have been sympathetic to other feminist causes—to join with conservatives. It also helps economic conservatives to achieve legitimacy in debates about women's issues. To emphasize this point, in the next section I show how IWF frames its concerns about violence against women in terms of women's interests, a move that helps establish it as an organization that stands for women.

Women's Interests

IWF considers itself to be a women's organization and, as demonstrated in chapter 3, engages in strategies to position itself as an institution that speaks for women. In accounts of its work on violence against women, then, IWF seeks to be clear that it has women's concerns at heart. Specifically, it claims to empower women by not casting them as victims of men or the state. Wholly consistent, too, with its economic conservative ideology, the image of "woman" that IWF wants to promote is that of a person whose decisions are unfettered by government intervention and feminist ideology. She is a smart, savvy woman, who can make up her own mind. For example, in summarizing a judge's interpretation of a California domestic violence law, IWF's Satel conveys the organization's belief that many domestic violence policies override women's individual freedoms:

> The California legislature has made it mandatory for judges to issue a restraining order separating the parties in all domestic violence cases. "It's ridiculous," the judge says of this mandatory separation, "each situation is different." Sometimes a woman doesn't want the separation, particularly if the threat from her husband is mild. "If the woman feels relatively safe, she might well rather have her kids' father home with the family," Judge Cannon says. In California, however, this option is no longer open to women. As Judge Cannon says, "We treat women as brainless individuals who are unable to make choices. If a woman wants a restraining order, she can ask us for it."[42]

Satel, a psychiatrist and Yale University professor, proceeds to argue in favor of the judge's perspective, suggesting that state intervention can have the effect of undermining women's abilities to make independent decisions.

IWF also cautions that domestic violence programs that encourage women to leave their partners interfere with women taking responsibility for their part in bad relationships. For IWF, self-determination goes hand in hand with personal accountability. Focusing only on men's actions in domestic violence situations, IWF alleges, may deter women from obtaining help or changing their behavior. Additionally, IWF criticizes programs for battered women because they can encourage women to leave their batterers instead of giving them the "choice" to work through their problems with their partners and reconcile their differences. The organization sees this as an affront to women's capacities to make their own decisions about relationships and marriage. In these cases, IWF considers itself to be acting in the interests of women, that is, allowing women to determine for themselves what their interests are. Of course, there is a tension here, as IWF is working with policymakers and the media to help define women's interests as the organization itself sees them. Still, IWF contends that feminist interpretations are premised on a narrow and skewed understanding of women's lives and that its alternative conceptualizations better suit the lives of most women.

In the case of domestic violence, IWF also tries to widen its appeal to women by talking about the interests of battered women living on welfare. Since conservative organizations in general have been charged with neglecting poor women or, even worse, demonizing them,[43] IWF's speaking to the needs of women living in poverty can help conservatives to counter the claim that they do not care about this class of citizen. In 1996, federal legislation was amended[44] so that battered women who sought welfare could be exempted from time restrictions and work requirements. Supporters of the exemption noted that many women on welfare are victims of domestic violence. Because victims of domestic violence often have to leave their homes and jobs while still supporting a child, advocates argued that new welfare provisions could be especially punitive to women trying to escape violent relationships. Thus, feminists and other activists pushed hard to get the provision passed. IWF, however, believes that such exemptions hurt poor women by encouraging men to keep up the abuse:

> If anything, the amendment puts abused women at even greater risk by turning these women into cash cows for their deadbeat lovers. Consider: a mother and her children are living with a shiftless lout who sponges off her government check, food stamps, and Section 8 apartment. He learns that battered women can keep getting their benefits. If keeping his partner brutalized means a regular check for him, some men will do just that.[45]

IWF's depiction of men in these cases differs from its portrayal of men who are not poor and displays a class bias in the organization's perspective. As noted, the organization tries to motivate women to think about saving their marriages and criticizes feminists for being antimale. In the case of poor women whose partners are batterers, the message is different. Men in this case are cast as "shiftless louts" who are not worth holding on to, indicating that the organization believes that poor women and men need to make different decisions than middle- and upper-income people because of their class status.

IWF also ties its support for women on welfare to its economic conservative assessment of welfare programs. Generally, IWF favors welfare reform that shifts control from the federal to state governments, and it opposes policies that call for subsidizing poor mothers who do not work outside the home. Consistent with its emphasis on self-sufficiency and financial independence, the organization alleges that exempting battered women from welfare regulations runs counter to their interests because it discourages them from leaving the welfare rolls. In some ways, tying its criticism of welfare into domestic violence allows IWF to issue a double whammy to feminists. It declares that feminists are not only misguided when it comes to helping battered women, but also suggests that feminists care little about the interests of poor women—a serious claim that has been leveled by others against feminists.

IWF also expresses its concern for women's interests in the case of sexual harassment. Since it was born in part from a group of women who called themselves Women for Judge Thomas, IWF has a legacy of challenging feminist interpretations and advocacy of sexual harassment policies. In 1991, Clarence Thomas, now a U.S. Supreme Court justice, faced a bitter and contested nomination for his seat in that chamber. The infamous hearings generated much attention when it was revealed that Anita Hill accused Thomas of sexually harassing her when she worked for him at the Equal Employment Opportunity Commission. As noted in Chapter Two, one-time IWF board president Ricky Silberman worked as Thomas's vice chair at the EEOC, was his friend and champion, and helped to organize Women for Judge Thomas.

IWF does not oppose sexual harassment policies per se. It is the scope of the laws that troubles the organization, and it believes that feminist organizations have gone too far in defining the behaviors that constitute harassment. For their part, feminists[46] have long argued that women should be protected against sexual harassment by policies that outlaw sexual discrimination in the workplace. Through feminist advocacy, sexual harassment has been legally defined as "the imposition of unwelcome sexual demands or the creation of sexually offensive environments."[47] When unwelcome sexual demands are tied into the victim's job benefits, the behavior is referred to as *quid pro quo harassment*. The second type of infraction, where workplace surroundings or conditions can be construed as harmful and thus as interfering with an employee's ability to do her job, falls under the category of *hostile environment harassment*. As a result of feminist efforts, many employers have adopted training policies for their employees and instituted guidelines meant to educate workers about what falls under the rubric of sexual harassment. This is due in part to the fact that employers can be found liable in sexual harassment cases.

Although, in its early years, IWF suffered some internal disagreement over where it should stand on the issue of sexual harassment, it is now more focused. Specifically, IWF supports sanctions against quid pro quo harassment. Conversely, it is much more skeptical of hostile environment claims, in which a person can argue that a coworker's conduct has created an intimidating, hostile, or offensive workplace. Generally, the organization contends that women's interests are not served by hostile environment sexual harassment policies because such laws disable women from acting on amorous feelings or even, sometimes, being bawdy. Women, the organization argues, want to flirt, be romantic, and have a little fun. As Christine Stolba, an IWF research fellow, told me: "There are legitimate hostile environment claims...but we need to be more realistic about it, especially in the narrower [sense], you know, where men and women meet and fall in love in the office almost as often as they harass each other. Women trade body jokes just like men."[48] Stolba (now Rosen), a working professional with a Ph.D. in history, then adds: "but that goes back to our [position that] women shouldn't be victims, they should be made of sterner stuff."

Overreaching sexual harassment laws not only constrain women's desires and actions, they also hurt women's employment possibilities, according to IWF. The organization contends that employers will be hesitant to hire women because they fear dealing with sexual harassment claims. Feminists have argued that sexual discrimination laws should include protection from sexual harassment; IWF argues that some sexual harassment laws will lead to employment discrimination. Although the latter is illegal, it does make for a compelling claim and one that could convince women to be wary of sexual harassment policies and feminist advocacy.

As the analyses presented in this section indicate, IWF does seek to speak to the interests of women. It takes a risk by denouncing laws like VAWA, but it is firm in its conviction that to help women is to empower them—by emphasizing women's decision-making capabilities. Its women's interests frames are meant to transform understandings of violence against women from feminist articulations to ones more consistent with IWF's views. For example, it argues that sexual harassment and domestic violence programs supported by feminists are antithetical to women's self-determination. In so doing, IWF constructs feminists as the enemy of women's individual freedom, essentially turning feminist messages about women's liberation on their head. As I will demonstrate in the next section, IWF's interpretation of established violence against women policies also rests on its economic conservative beliefs and its preference for limited government involvement in personal matters and business affairs.

No Thank You, Uncle Sam

True to its economic conservative roots, IWF argues that federal antiviolence laws create obstacles for women who wish to realize their own potential freedom from government interference. It contends that feminist policies regarding domestic violence, date rape, and sexual harassment not only promote feminism and scare women, but also waste tax dollars, enable "big government," and hurt businesses—all concerns of economic conservatives. Summing up the current organizational position on sexual harassment, Stolba told me:

> I do think there is not a single person in the organization who would say that we shouldn't have legal protections for quid pro quo harassment, which was always the intent.... Now most of the cases filed at the EEOC are hostile environment claims, not quid pro quo claims.... Well, now they are half, times have changed, so that the underlying theory behind certainly MacKinnon's[49] work was again this idea that sexual harassment is just one form of men's subordination of women society wide. That is what we have a problem with. Our argument is [that] most men are not harassers. But if they do harass an employee, they had better well be punished. But let's not go overboard, let's not have draconian speech codes and all this other stuff.[50]

As Stolba's comments and my subsequent analyses will reveal, IWF alleges that feminists have gone too far in trying to involve the government in regulating interpersonal behaviors.

With regard to domestic violence, IWF takes issue with the VAWA federal civil rights clause because it believes that the provision diverts power from the states and adds bureaucratic layers to the law enforcement process. Instead, IWF argues that the personal safety of women would be best secured by holding state and local authorities responsible for the prosecution of violent crimes. This conviction was articulated in a press release announcing IWF's filing of an amicus brief in *U.S. v. Morrison*:

> With the implementation of VAWA, Congress chose to establish a pointless and redundant "right" to sue attackers in federal, as well as state, court. In its amicus curiae brief filed in this case, the Independent Women's Forum argues that Congress is wasting its time—and adding to victims' suffering—by federalizing offenses already prohibited by state laws.[51]

Its statement to the press implies that the organization not only considers VAWA to be a way to indoctrinate women with feminist values, but is also a means to increase the powers of the federal government. As such, it violates IWF's economic conservative preference for states' rights approaches to social problems.

On the topic of sexual harassment laws, IWF opposes allowing for hostile environment claims on the grounds that such policies hurt businesses by forcing them to hire consultants to establish proper protocols for employees. The expansion of sexual harassment laws, according to IWF, may also encourage female employees to see being sexually harassed as one way to extract money or other resources from their employers. As IWF author Elizabeth Larson argued:

> Like the college students persuaded by their feminist sisters that an unwanted kiss is really rape, today's businesswomen are being taught that behavior they once would have considered boorish or inappropriate constitutes actionable sexual harassment. Employers may think they are hiring consultants to protect them from lawsuits, but what is actually being taught is a very different lesson: a wink or a leer can be money in the bank.[52]

IWF's defense of business suggests a tension between the organization's support for women's interests and its affirmation that corporations and the like should be free from government regulation. One could argue that, based on Larson's observations, IWF has little faith in women. That is, it believes that women will be easily swayed by laws and policies, even if the policies are not ultimately in their best interests. However, because the organization does artfully juxtapose its narratives with those that chastise feminists and also speaks to women's interests, it manages to convey a sense of caring and concern for women, suggesting that corporate and women's interests are interrelated, not oppositional. This helps to broaden the scope of economic conservatism, rendering it an ideological point of view that specifically encompasses the needs of women.

IWF also meshes antifeminist frames with its concerns about excessive taxation. Contrasting antifeminist and economic conservative narratives makes feminists appear self-interested and eager to cash in on women's perceived vulnerability. IWF bemoans that, through VAWA, people are spending tax dollars to indoctrinate women into "profeminist" treatment programs. Former IWF health policy fellow Sally Satel suggests that VAWA is a feminist boondoggle "used to further an ideological war against men—one that puts many women at even greater risk."[53]

Its criticism of federal government spending extends to the subject of a VAWA-funded national domestic violence hotline. IWF's Kimberly Schuld writes of this telephone service that "a woman who is being beaten needs the local cops, not tea and sympathy from someone thousands of miles away." The hotline, she alleges, is a waste of government funding.[54]

Like many feminist organizations, IWF tackles the issue of violence against women. But its eagerness to dispel feminist claims and to highlight violence against men has brought about criticism of its goals and mission.[55] Nonetheless, from its perspective, the organization is helping women—to challenge the negative consequences of feminist ideology, to make their own decisions about relationships and workplace protocols, and to be free from overbearing state intervention. Given the political context and IWF's goal of establishing itself as a credible representative of women's interests, all of these pieces fit well together.

CONCLUSIONS

In the case of violence against women, IWF is more reactionary and specifically antifeminist than is CWA. CWA expresses its concerns about women and its social conservative values about gender roles, sexuality, and culture through its opposition to pornography. Here, the organization presents arguments that parallel some feminists but also resonate with its social conservative base, especially as it contends that pornography disrupts traditional conceptualizations of home and family life. This complicates our understanding of the divide between feminist and conservative women, suggesting the necessity for exploring women's issues with attention to context, strategy, and nuance.

Indeed, there have been cases, as in the fight for passage of the 1983 Minneapolis ordinance, where both social conservatives and feminists supported placing restrictions on access to pornography.

IWF talks about violence, but not about violence qua violence. Its mission with regard to this issue is premised on the need to take on feminist legislation and feminist definitions of policy goals and transform them to fit with its economic conservative values. And for now, conservatives with institutional power are paying attention to IWF. Its former president, Nancy Pfotenhauer, and one of its national advisory board members, Margot Hill, were appointed by President George W. Bush to serve on the Justice Department's National Advisory Commission on Violence against Women. This body was created through the passage of VAWA to monitor the act's execution and to advise Justice Department officials. IWF saw this as "a unique opportunity to work with the Administration in changing the attitudes and perceptions surrounding domestic violence, sexual assault, and stalking,"[56] while feminist groups like NOW urged members to write letters of protest about the appointments. Clearly, the organization and its leaders are being taken seriously by other conservatives with political influence, although it is not evident that their presence greatly influenced implementation of VAWA, since they failed to sway lawmakers to change the bill when it came up for renewal. Some of IWF's goals were met, however, when the U.S. Supreme Court handed down its ruling in *U.S. v. Morrison*.

Tempting as it may be for feminists to dismiss the women of CWA and IWF as "pod feminists,"[57] conservative women should not be underestimated in terms of their efforts to influence political agendas. For some women and men, hearing about women's issues through ideological lenses other than feminism may be compelling, changing the way they perceive conservatism, how the broader movement attends to women's issues, and the policy solutions offered by groups like CWA and IWF.

Chapter 5

FINDING COMMON GROUND
Constructing Mothers' Interests

NEWSPAPERS, BOOKS, AND magazines trumpet headlines about the "mommy wars": women fighting with each over who constitute better parents—mothers who stay at home with their children or those who choose to remain in the paid workforce. Whether these conflicts are real or hyped, they reflect actual concerns about women's familial and social roles, government's place in providing child care services, and the tensions felt by parents, especially mothers, about the conflicting needs of the home and workplace. Feminist organizations have sought to respond to these issues by advocating for policies like the Pregnancy Discrimination Act, Family and Medical Leave Act, and federal funding for child care. Although meeting with limited success, feminists have managed to prompt lawmakers to take these issues more seriously. As women's organizations, CWA and IWF also seek to address women's unhappiness with government and employer attention to family strife by entering into these debates, offering their interpretations of the problems and proposing policy solutions. Unlike the issue of violence against women, where CWA and IWF express differing views on the role of government and the relative influence of feminism, here CWA and IWF seem to have found common ground. On the topic of mothers' interests, the organizations offer narratives that can help to bridge the divide among women within the conservative movement. To examine how these conservative players address the subject of mothers' interests, in this chapter I will explore what it looks like when two ideologically distinct conservative organizations articulate similar narratives as they seek to establish themselves as representatives of women's interests.

On the issue of mothers' interests, CWA is less likely to call for state intervention than it is on other issues, like violence against women. It alleges that too much federal government involvement in workplace policies geared toward families supersedes parental authority and harms children. Here, it shares a mission with IWF in calling for a laissez-faire approach to family life.[1] Conversely, IWF is willing in the case of mothers' interests to play up gender role differences between men and women and argue that these distinctions stem from biological factors. Like its social conservative counterpart, IWF argues that women have naturally born maternal instincts and are generally better suited than men to be primary caregivers. As such, there is overlap between the two groups with regard to their rhetoric about mothers' interests. While their narratives merge with one another, they also fit well within each organization's specific conservative ideologies, as will be discussed. Their articulating common beliefs about mothers' interests also points to the fluidity between social and economic conservatism and suggests that these groups should be able to coalesce on some key policy items.

We know that when social and economic conservatives use common language to debate issues, such "fusionism" positively affects their ability to shape political outcomes and public policies.[2] Diamond documents examples where economic conservatives have strategized with social conservatives, formed coalitions, and/or presented unified messages to policymakers and the public.[3] For example, she notes that economic conservative leader Paul Weyrich was responsible for suggesting the use of the phrase "pro-family"[4] that so many social conservative organizations have adopted. Others find similar results, arguing that mounting pressure to work with established political parties and to defeat liberal candidates encourages social and economic conservatives to craft coherent campaigns and messages.[5] These scholars emphasize the central and profound role of fusionism in building and maintaining conservative movements. In looking at how CWA and IWF frame mothers' interests, evidence of shared rhetoric is abundant. Since women bring different issues and ways of participating to politics, it is important to understand not only how these groups speak about motherhood, but what they contribute to the process of fusionism within the conservative movement as well.

As with violence against women issues, CWA and IWF rely on the same three frames—antifeminist, social/economic conservative, and women's interests—to speak as organizations representing mothers. Their public pronouncements reveal that the organizations recognize that many women feel conflicted about work and family issues and that feminists have made some progress in addressing and defining these concerns. Nonetheless, while feminists have tapped into women's concerns and have been at the helm in defining these issues for women, lawmakers and businesses have been generally resistant to their ideas. There is no national policy for paid family leave, and few child care facilities receive substantial government assistance. Thus, as CWA and IWF speak to conservatives by evoking nostalgic maternal images that rarely threaten traditional conceptualizations of gender role norms, they have solid institutional support on their side. And, as conservative women proclaiming these views, they play a unique and decidedly critical role in a process that constructs public meanings about motherhood and the role of women in families and the workforce.

WHY MOTHERS' INTERESTS?

Before moving on, it is important to note the significance of mothers' interests to both organizations and the meaning this subject has for conservative and feminist politics. As an organization prone to libertarian views about government involvement in social and economic affairs, IWF is disinclined to engage in debates about abortion, homosexuality, and pornography. As I discussed earlier, these issues are central to the mission of the social conservative CWA. Other women's issues, like pay equity policies and violence against women, are on IWF's front burner, but are not highlighted by CWA because of its decision to focus on more social conservative issues. Concerns about mothering, on the other hand, are fundamental to both organizations. Speaking to the needs of women with children fits well within both organizations' ideological parameters and does not conflict with the goals of either one.

Motherhood is also a key category of contestation between feminists and conservatives. As Annelise Orleck reminds us, debates about motherhood have played a central role in conservative politics in the United States and elsewhere. "Bad mothers" are blamed for a "culture's descent into chaos," while "good mothers" are necessary to restore order and civility.[6] Bad mothers work full time and buy into feminist messages about "having it all," while good mothers center their lives around child rearing and domestic labor. Through debates about the marital status of mothers on welfare, the acceptability of women with children working outside the home, and the role of the maternal body in reproductive health controversies, activists and policymakers have argued over what constitutes the ideal mother and have helped to define her image. Clashes over motherhood and child care policies also reflect wider ideological debates over women's familial, political, and economic status, foregrounding deeper divisions over gender roles and the functions of personal and institutional power.[7] Engaging in debates over motherhood enables CWA and IWF to speak to the needs of women who are attempting to balance work and family life, while reinforcing conservative political messages about what constitutes ideal mothering.

A NOTE ABOUT MOTHERHOOD AND INTERVIEWEES

In the following sections, I demonstrate that CWA and IWF sing the praises of stay-at-home motherhood. Nonetheless, all but one of my interviewees are women who work outside of the home. Some of them have small children, while many have older children or none at all. When I inquired of these leaders if there were women with children working at their organizations, they related that those who did tried to work from home or part time. I also asked interviewees to respond to the stereotype that conservative organizations like theirs "encourage women to be homemakers." All of their answers were similar: they maintained that they were merely trying to increase options for women by creating a social and political climate that values stay-at-home mothering. As this chapter discusses, according to CWA and IWF, feminists are to be blamed for limiting women's choices and making mothers think that they have to be "superwomen" to be successful and happy.

Several IWF interviewees also acknowledged that, for many women, figuring out compromises between their work and family was actually more appealing than choosing to permanently leave the workforce. Some suggested that women would be happiest if they chose full- or part-time stay-at-home motherhood for a few years and then planned on returning to the paid workforce to build their careers. And several of these advocates admitted to the challenges of staying home full time with children. As one IWF board member confides:

So let us be honest about it. I personally would lose my mind if I had to do play-doh all day. I think that we in some ways do value motherhood more than feminists certainly did. Some of them, like Betty Friedan, in their evolution, have come around to say that they value it more than they did. But there was certainly a feeling in the 1970s and '80s that feminists by and large didn't care about, and devalued, being a mother who stayed at home. I admire women that can do it, I simply do not have the self-discipline or whatever it takes to endure that all day long. I don't know many women who do.[8]

Similarly, a CWA staff member relates these thoughts about the appeal of working outside of the home:

The role of a homemaker, especially if they're a mother, it never ends, seven days a week, twenty-four hours a day. So I have the utmost respect for homemakers, and I know the rest of the women here do too. But that being said, we believe that women are very capable of letting their opinions be known, are capable of running an organization, are capable of being players in the political process, and very well should be. So while we value homemakers, we also value women being in the workplace.[9]

To mitigate the contradictions inherent between their professional lives and the lives of the constituency of mothers for whom they claim to speak, both organizations combine attacks on feminism with positive rhetoric about motherhood. Like feminists, they view their work as increasing opportunities for women and making them feel valued. And, unlike women who opposed suffrage, these conservative women are comfortable promoting the idea that opting out of the paid workforce does not mean women should be excluded from the "public" life of politics.

While one-on-one, my interviewees produced a more nuanced and complicated assessment of the relationship between mothering and the workplace, organizational publications and policy positions consistently frame mothers' interests in much more narrow and definitive ways. This glorification of motherhood is a framing strategy that could help them speak to more women. Even women who enjoy working outside the home can appreciate the exaltation of motherhood, as it urges people to take women's work more seriously. In addition, as I will demonstrate in the following sections, the mothers' interest frames reinforce conservative views about family dynamics and structures and promote conservative conceptualizations about the role of government. In so doing, their rhetoric about motherhood and public policy gives them credibility among this important group of allies.

CONSTRUCTING MOTHERS' INTERESTS

The Ideal Mother

At the heart of CWA's and IWF's debates about mothers' interests lies an idealized image of motherhood or what it means to be maternal. Here, the organizations converge in message, as they argue that women's goals as mothers are biologically derived. Like feminists, they call for attention to women's anxieties about working and motherhood, but contend that tensions between the two arise when women deny their natural desires to be stay-at-home mothers in order to seek professional success and/or earn more money for their families. They blame this disconnect on feminism and on the failure of policymakers to pass laws that increase the take-home income of families.

According to Sharon Hays, women's beliefs about what kind of parents they should be are motivated by the "ideology of intensive mothering."[10] Hays argues that this thinking comes from the social construction of appropriate child rearing and is grounded in the belief that women should be the main caregivers and put their children's needs above their own. She finds this child-centered approach promoted by parenting books and espoused, albeit with qualifications, by the mothers she interviewed. Due to social pressures to conform to this standard, Hays argues, mothers employed outside of the home experience stress and anxiety, regardless of their political values and independent of their economic status.[11] Hays's overall assessment provides important insights into understanding feminist evaluations of the tensions working mothers feel. For example, feminists are critical of employers who fail to accommodate working families by offering child care and/or adequate leave benefits. For feminists, the "intensive mother" is a destructive social construct, setting up unrealistic expectations for women.

CWA and IWF, however, embrace the notion of intensive mothering but argue that feminism and liberal economic policies create discord by encouraging women to work when they would be happiest staying home caring for their young children. This locates both organizations in a common space and in an ideological field distinct from feminism. It also gives women a reason to support conservative interpretations of mothers' interests. As put forth by CWA and IWF, women wanting to be intensive mothers is natural and involves recognizing that young children need their mothers to be at home with them. Intensive mothers are willing to make material and personal sacrifices to fulfill their maternal duties. While some interviewees conceded that women should be free to choose between stay-at-home mothering or entering the paid workforce, most of their organizations' public rhetoric involves framing mothers' interests in a way that encourages women to stay at home when their children are young. Such reasoning is couched in terms of gender differences—that it is more natural for women to want to be their children's primary caretakers and that it is better for children to be with their mothers.

The promotion of organic gender differences between men and women undergirds both organizations' claims that women require public policies to help them fulfill their quest to be at-home parents. This sentiment is well exemplified by CWA founder Beverly LaHaye, who argues: "most little girls will tell you that when they grow up they want to be mommies. There's nothing more natural."[12] A CWA staffer articulates this sentiment about women's "natural" proclivity toward mothering: "I just think that women are natural nurturers and are more concerned about what's going on in the home; whereas a lot of time men are concerned about what is going on in the marketplace."[13] Providing a strikingly similar line of reasoning, IWF's Ricky Silberman relates this about women's roles as mothers:

> I think we have to recognize essential gender differences. I think that true feminism says that women are different than men, that women are just as good as men at whatever they try to do, and that women have to be intelligent about their choices of when they try to do what it is they are trying to do, and not turn their back on what is the most fulfilling and important role in society. That is, their roles as mother in a family.[14]

In addition to honoring the maternal instinct, CWA and IWF also argue that women are predisposed to be particular kinds of mothers: women who put their children's needs ahead of their own. According to IWF, a good mother "refuses to bow to social forces telling her . . . to continue 'putting children last.'"[15] Like IWF, CWA charges: "you sacrifice your time, your energy and your own desires. . . . You go without luxuries so they can have necessities—and you don't complain." This, it professes, is the "Power of Motherhood."[16] When a woman leaves her career (and income), she is realizing her own maternal interests.

In fact, both organizations express sympathy for women who feel they "have" to work and thus suppress their "natural" desires. They recognize that many women feel conflicted about wanting or having to work versus staying home with their children. Nonetheless, they suggest that this tension stems from the conflict between women's maternal instincts and the feminist insistence that she suppress it to get a job. Neither cite lack of partner support nor employer ignorance as causes for these personal struggles.

Both organizations also conflate parenting with mothering, a rhetorical move that reinforces the notion that women are more fit than men to be primary caretakers. With the exception of one article written about the experiences of a stay-at-home father,[17] there is little talk about fathers' interests in discussions about child care. True, fathers are presumed to be concerned about their children, but they are not considered to be conflicted about their employment status or driven to be a child's primary caretaker. To be clear, not all of the women interviewed from the two organizations think women must be stay-at-home mothers. However, even those interviewees who had young children and were themselves in the paid workforce argued that women are better equipped than men to take care of children, when a choice could be made. As CWA put it in a headline about the alleged negative effects of child care centers: "Nothing Can Replace Mom's Care."[18] And, in criticizing an article that put a salary value on the work of stay-at-home mothers, IWF retorted:

> But placing a number on a mom's value misses the point. Women perform these duties because they love their families. Moms aren't daycare providers worth $14 per hour—they are loving parents driven to care for those tiny beings who are more precious to them than any amount of money. Serving as your child's "psychologist" and your home's "facility manager" isn't work—it's the essence of life. Your compensation isn't measured in dollars, but in building a life that you love.[19]

Both IWF and CWA speak about mothers' interests in ways that reflect social conservative views of gender differences and familial responsibilities. For CWA, framing gender differences as natural is consistent with its overall organizational ideology. For IWF, however, with its economic conservative belief in individual choice, one might expect less emphasis on women's differences from men. However, making claims that women are biologically distinct from men is not inconsistent with IWF's views. In fact, it asserts that, because women are naturally different from men, women's individual decisions and choices will differ from men's as well. Thus, it actually broadens the scope of economic conservatism to argue that gender differences should have a central place in understanding the occupational and familial status of women and men. Like other economic conservatives, it shifts the debate away from social, economic, and/or political structures to focus instead on individual preferences. But, by also making claims about gender roles, it fuses its narratives with those of its social conservative counterpart. By drawing on the biological basis of mothering and appealing to women who believe that their true value lies in their roles as mothers, the organizations offer what could be compelling messages to a broad swath of the American female public. And here, the symbolic good mother acts as a unifying theme for these two organizations as they seek to speak for women and to establish conservatives as legitimate representatives of mothers' interests.

Opposition to Feminism

Data indicate that the majority of women who have children participate in the paid workforce.[20] Public opinion polls, however, suggest a great degree of ambivalence among women as to mothers' roles and responsibilities and what policies best address the conflicts between employment and family needs. Eighty-five percent of women cited "child care" as a top priority for a women's movement; however, in that study, 74% of that same population wanted time off to care for family members.[21] In this case, women are clearly expressing the need for help, but not necessarily a preference for day care over family leave. In another national poll, 68% of women said that "most women see a conflict between working and raising a family," as compared to the 28% who answered no to that question.[22] An earlier poll also found that 41% thought it was bad for mothers with young children to be in the workplace. In the same survey, 17% said it was a good thing, and 37% claimed that it did not make a difference.[23]

To some extent, feminists have attempted to negotiate between the needs of "home" life and the workplace by advocating for policies that enable parents to have careers while raising their children. They have sought and continue to seek workplace changes and government support to address the tensions that parents, especially mothers, face as they try to simultaneously raise children, have careers, and earn money.[24] These efforts include advocating for bills such as the Pay Equity Act, Pregnancy Discrimination Act, Act for Better Child Care, and Family and Medical Leave Act (FMLA). Some have met with more success than others.[25] Lawmakers have been more willing, for example, to support narrow initiatives like the unpaid family leave guaranteed by FMLA and less eager to fund broad-reaching programs like comprehensive child care or paid time off for parents. This stems in part from successful opposition by employers and businesses that have lobbied against government-regulated benefits.

It is incumbent upon CWA and IWF to acknowledge the gravity of the problem as perceived by women as well as the degree to which feminists have successfully tapped into women's concerns and advocated on their behalf. As I noted in chapter 1, a majority of women support the "women's movement," but many are ambivalent about "feminism" and being associated with the term. In seeking to appeal to a wide range of women, CWA and IWF expertly exploit this tension. They chastise feminist organizations for their advocacy of child care policies at the expense of stay-at-home mothers and cite the alleged pervasiveness of feminist ideology as one cause of mothers' dissatisfaction with their lives. The construction of feminism as a viable political and ideological threat to mothering is essential for these women's organizations to explain why so many women work outside the home and deny their own interests. It also helps these groups to construct their identities as organizations that really care about mothers' interests.

For CWA's part, feminism is cited as causing the degradation of motherhood and the rise in the number of children in poor-quality day care. An example of this sentiment is offered by CWA's founder, Beverly LaHaye:

> Look carefully at what feminists are promoting, and you will see that only one thing is considered: what the woman wants....In this warped view of motherhood, the child's needs are not even mentioned. *Motherhood* used to be a term of honor and responsibility; today it has been reduced to an optional status with an ever-decreasing sphere of influence.[26]

Like the social conservative LaHaye, IWF editor Danielle Crittenden offered a similar antifeminist frame to guide her readers through a special issue of the organization's magazine, *Women's Quarterly*, which was devoted to the topic of motherhood and child care: "In this special issue on motherhood, we offer our readers an unabashed defense of those women who dare to defy the feminist wisdom on which they were weaned and raised, to wean and raise their children themselves."[27] According to *Women's Quarterly* contributor Mona Charen, this feminist wisdom so criticized by Crittenden "has been at war with human nature from the beginning, and nowhere more so than its fierce campaign against motherhood."[28] Charen's comments closely echo those of CWA president Pate as she ponders feminism's relationship to the destruction of the traditional family:

> [T]he feminist movement has broken down what we believe is the traditional family, one man married to one woman, and fulfilling the roles that we feel that God has led them to fill in the home. We believe in the context of what God has laid out for men and women that creates the strongest environment for children; where both the mother and the father are equal in the home, yet they have different roles.[29]

Although some feminists have been critical of the institutions of marriage and motherhood, these conservative women's organizations' portrayal of their positions is oversimplified. Several interviewees cited Betty Friedan's *The Feminine Mystique*[30] as the quintessential text through which feminists have learned to degrade motherhood. Friedan's work did hit a nerve for many a housewife who felt unchallenged, overwhelmed, and underappreciated, but she and other feminists are hardly to blame for the devaluation of motherhood. Feminists have argued for years that "housework" and reproduction should be considered to be valuable forms of labor and experience.[31] True, some feminists, like Firestone,[32] have argued that reproduction and motherhood are sources of oppression for women, but many feminists have used and continue to use motherhood to make claims about women's worth and common experiences. Organizations like MomsRising.org, for example, call on mothers to organize collectively for "family-friendly" policies. Unlike conservative women, however, feminists blame sexism for the degradation of motherhood.

Nevertheless, both conservative women's organizations insist that feminists are narcissists and women who, at the expense of their children and partners, strive for personal gain and happiness. Feminism as an ideology is indicted for promoting self-centeredness and views allegedly antithetical to good mothering. For example, in an essay for IWF, Melinda Ledden Sidak likens the children of employed women to pets:

> Given the finite number of hours in the day, it seems curious that so many busy professionals do not consider the ease, practicality, and warm companionship of a dog or cat rather than the insatiable demands of children.... When they don't have time to care for Junior personally, which is in fact, most of the time, they have to hire a baby-sitter to

do the job for them, just as Fido's owner will hire a professional dog walker and pet-sitter. If they can't afford the personal in-home touch, they can just drop Junior off at the kennel—er, day-care center.... The parent loves Junior, just as Fido's owner loves Fido. But neither would dream of sacrificing important personal and professional aspirations because Fido and Junior would like more quality time at the park.[33]

Such condemnation of feminism does beg the question: if women's desires to be stay-at-home mothers are so natural, then how have feminists been so successful in getting women to suppress or undermine their instincts? According to CWA and IWF, feminist ideology overwhelmingly pervades public institutions like schools, government, and the media. Thus, women are not offered viable images of what true motherhood should look like. Nor do they feel that they have the choice to leave their jobs to be stay-at-home mothers. A major allegation by both CWA and IWF is that feminism has made it unpopular for women to be valued "solely" as mothers. Thus, women will deny their "maternal instincts" to seek satisfaction from their careers and material gain, only to find that, in the long run, they are unhappy. Feminists, according to CWA and IWF, have duped women and failed to acknowledge that mothers who work outside the home may be subject to malaise and unhappiness. One contributor to an IWF publication, who gave up her professional job to be a stay-at-home mother, writes that she and her friends are all happy, former professionals. She contends that she and other mothers who opted out of the workplace "understand more about real human interaction and deep emotional fulfillment than the cranky feminists who tut-tut that we're wasting our potential, 'giving up our lives,' and generally lounging around having pedicures."[34] Gurdon proceeds to condemn feminists for destroying the pride and satisfaction that many "housewives" enjoy. She encourages women to "show our daughters how admirable and richly rewarding it can be not to spend all day at the office."[35]

For decades, feminists have sought the implementation of policies that ameliorate the tensions that women (and men) face between working outside the home and raising children by lobbying for solutions to make employers and government officials more responsive to the needs of parents. To counteract feminist political efforts, CWA and IWF argue that what feminists are purposively doing is making mothers who forgo paid employment feel inadequate. They transform the meaning of "having it all" into a concept that allegedly shows feminists' contempt for women who choose to stay at home when their children are young. Along with their conservative partners, CWA and IWF blame feminists for insisting that the ideal woman is superwoman—she who parents and works outside the home. Feminist scholars document other sources of this imagery;[36] nonetheless, it has become commonplace for the feminist movement to be equated with the notion that stay-at-home mothers are failures. In response, CWA and IWF frame women's roles as wives and mothers as being sacred and sources of great pride for women. This imagery can be appealing to the millions of women who have chosen to leave the paid workforce, but it can also undermine feminist policy efforts to raise federal funds for day care centers or to broaden the scope of the FMLA. It also influences reproductive health debates that center around the role of women vis-à-vis their fetuses, by allowing policymakers to advance the notion that a pregnant woman's first responsibility is to her "unborn child."[37]

In the case of mothers' interests, this mutual framing of feminism in negative terms produces several outcomes. It targets feminism as the source of women's problems and positions CWA and IWF as alternative organizations for women to support and join. As noted, this can weaken feminist intervention into child care and other policies directed at working families. It also enables CWA and IWF to have a distinct role in policy contests between feminists and conservatives. Coming from their male counterparts, condemnation of feminism can sound paternalistic and thus may not be taken as seriously by the public or lawmakers. As articulated by both social and economic conservative women, however, antifeminist frames can help to legitimate the conservative movement and its positions on how best to address mothers' interests. It may also link women to other conservative groups and policy efforts.[38]

What Should Government Do?

For CWA and IWF, in a perfect world, there would be little need for child care. Women would not "need" to work and would have the flexibility to stay home with their children until they are at least of school age. However, these conservative women's organizations are aware that many women do work outside of the home and some enjoy it; thus, as women's organizations seeking to be taken seriously by a range of women, they must speak to this audience. Although each group expresses a preference for policies that enable women to choose stay-at-home mothering, given the reality of women's lives and the influence of feminism in opening up career and economic opportunities for women (including themselves), CWA and IWF also support solutions that attend to the needs of women who work outside the home. Both groups are especially sympathetic to single mothers who have no husband to support them. They are not, however, supportive of women who "choose" single motherhood from the onset. When they express sympathy for single mothers, they are referring to widows or to women whose husbands have left them. However, they do support "workfare" programs and subsidized child care for poor women on welfare, indicating a class bias in their appreciation for which women should be stay-at-home parents.

Here, we see how CWA and IWF merge their respective social and economic conservative frames and thus articulate values and goals that are consistent with each other. For example, while CWA is explicit about its social conservative fear of government forcing liberal beliefs on families, it also argues that government-funded child care is wasteful to taxpayers, an economic conservative argument. One CWA staffer likens institutionalized child care to socialism, suggesting the imposition of both government (im)morality and an oppressive economic system on unwilling citizens:

> I think that as a parent it concerns me that just more and more rights are being taken away from parents and put into the hands of government. It is a very socialistic philosophy, particularly if you look at the child care issue; the desire to truly take children at the earliest ages, as early as three months, to put them in government-controlled day care centers so they can be not taught the values and beliefs of their parents, but the values and beliefs of government. I think that is a very dangerous trend that we seem to be heading to in our society.[39]

Not surprisingly, the economic conservatives of IWF cite fiscal concerns when talking about child care policies. For CWA, this emphasis indicates a willingness to engage narratives more frequently associated with economic conservatives and to merge their arguments with those of their conservative sisters. It does contradict CWA's call for government intervention into other social issues like abortion and school prayer, but this uneasy relationship with the state has been an issue for the conservative movement for decades without doing it significant damage.[40] While this position may generate criticism for its inconsistencies, it also allows CWA to show that a social conservative organization has the ability to reach out to conservatives beyond its membership base. Since fusionism has facilitated conservative activism on other issues, it is likely to help conservative women get this message out as well.

The economic conservative women of IWF frame government-funded day care to be an unnecessary taxpayer expense and one that would "crowd out private providers and...leave women with fewer child-care options."[41] But, IWF also expresses fear about the state's ability to instill liberal antifamily values into children and society as a whole. In so doing, the organization artfully bridges concerns about the denigration of capitalism with concerns about the devaluation of parents' roles. IWF's expression of anxiety about parental rights matches closely with statements made by CWA. This common rhetoric is well illustrated by one IWF author, as she suggests that the need for child care has been largely fabricated:

> [T]he best resolution Congress could adopt would be to stand back and allow parents, not politicians, to determine what is best for their children. Only parents are equipped to make decisions about what sort of care their children need. If politicians insist on doing something for children, they should simply cut taxes. Reducing taxes would help parents to be able to spend more time with their children, afford better child care, or do whatever it is they think best for their families.[42]

For both organizations, the way to lessen government intrusion into families, restore parental control, and reduce the need for child care is to offer tax reductions to families and employers, offer incentives to workplaces to allow parents to spend more time with their children, and encourage businesses to adopt flex-time policies. For example, in 2004, both organizations came out in favor of President George W. Bush's proposal to amend the Fair Labor Standards Act to allow employees to swap overtime pay for comp time, arguing that this would allow working women to use stored hours to spend time with their children. NOW and other feminist organizations opposed this change on the grounds that it really serves businesses by allowing them to reclassify employees once eligible for overtime into positions that offer comp time, a "perk" that is more difficult to use, especially for lower-income women. Feminist groups do welcome employer support for working parents, but have generally considered these types of policies to be weak alternatives to state-sponsored paid leave and subsidized child care because of a lack of employer cooperation and/or government enforcement. According to CWA and IWF, however, these practices improve the economic conditions that "force" many women to work. That is, tax cuts can relieve families of financial hardship, allowing women to stay home without sacrificing too much of the family's material necessities. Consistent with its ideology, IWF supports lowering taxes to facilitate women's ability to stay at home with young children full or part time. And, since the presidency of Ronald Reagan ushered in an era resplendent with calls for tax breaks, even among Democrats, calls for these solutions usually find a receptive audience among elected officials and their constituents.

Amending tax codes is also supported by CWA. Both organizations lobbied for a $500 per child tax break and take credit for working with U.S. senator Kay Bailey Hutchison (R-TX) to pass a Homemakers' IRA bill.[43] CWA president Carmen Pate notes the reasons for CWA's advocacy of these economic policies:

> A study that we did about a year ago pointed out that eight out of ten women, if they could financially afford to do so, would stay home and be mom. But our society has just not created an atmosphere for them to feasibly do that. So we are working to provide tax breaks for women so they can choose whether they are going to stay home or work or start their own in-home business or whatever.[44]

Through advocacy of these tax-based policy solutions, both organizations offer proposals that can be appealing to a range of conservatives and other citizens, therefore enabling them to speak to their constituencies and allies and to articulate policy goals that differ from those of feminists. Both address the concerns of women who fear the decline of moral values and the burden of high taxes, thus solidifying support among other conservative women and establishing themselves as women's representatives within the conservative movement. And each reaches out to the broader public of women who are looking for resolutions to the tensions they feel between child-rearing and workplace expectations, who have come of age in a political climate highly supportive of tax-reduction policies. Inasmuch as their frames are persuasive to this larger group of women, they can distinguish themselves as the women's organizations best able to champion mothers' interests to policymakers.

On the issue of child care and tax policy, there is little that separates CWA and IWF. As organizations advocating for women with children, there is clear evidence of fusionism between the groups' assessment of social problems and the laws proposed to ameliorate them. Through their unique contributions as women articulating unified messages on behalf of other women, CWA and IWF help to establish the broader conservative movement as one that cares about mothers and is unified in its ideas about what proposals work best for families.

CWA and IWF are not distinct in articulating ideas and policy solutions that bring together social and economic conservative values. They do, however, bring unique contributions as conservative women articulating shared narratives about mothers' interests. They provide legitimacy that men lack in this case, especially as many women feel that men do not understand the struggles they face in trying to balance work and family responsibilities. While men's domestic roles have changed over time to include their greater participation in household labor, women still take on more of the "second shift."[45]

This chapter, like those that have preceded it, shows how conservative women can shift and enlarge the boundaries of conservatism. This is especially true for IWF, as it brings to light the role of maternity as well as gender differences in economic conservative interpretations of workplace policies. To this end, the organization released a well-publicized report dismissing the existence of "glass ceilings" and the need for pay equity policies. It claimed and continues to argue that women's pay and managerial status need to be reconsidered in light of their choice to prioritize mothering.[46] In other words, women's and men's salary differentials are due to women taking time off to stay at home with children or choosing less-demanding work assignments that subsequently pay less. Consistent with its economic conservatism, IWF considers the wage outcomes to be premised on individual choices. But it also argues that the decisions themselves are influenced by the inherent differences between women and men.

That there is fusionism on mothers' interests between CWA and IWF has implications for conservative politics more widely. Although CWA and IWF do not usually work together, their mutual goals could compel them to do so. Even lacking such instrumentality, their unity in message has consequences. For the conservative movement, having ideologically distinct camps of women speak the same language on issues like child care could bolster its causes. As I discussed earlier, fusionism has had a profound and, from their perspective, positive impact on conservatives' abilities to mobilize support from a wide range of activists and the general public. Each organization could persuade different factions within the conservative movement to support the other's goals. That they agree on tax policies and maternal identities can send a strong message to other conservatives about the meaning of these issues and how best to debate them with opponents.

For conservative women, coherence on issues could prove to be the way to grow this fledgling conservative women's movement and, ultimately, affect the larger conservative movement. For example, CWA is exhibiting a willingness to engage in arguments consistent with the more "secular" side of the conservative movement—a strategy that could appeal to conservatives who have been wary of the religiosity of the Christian Right. As social conservatives seek alliances with their more secular counterparts and as they move to make inroads within the Republican Party,[47] being able to connect with economic conservatives could provide them with some legitimacy and additional access to political leaders. After all, IWF does boast Second Lady Lynne Cheney and Labor Secretary Elaine Chao among its advisory board members. For IWF's part, any ability to appeal to a grassroots organization like CWA could enhance its impact and, at the very least, enlarge its mailing list and donor base.

Chapter 6

REPRESENTING WOMEN'S HEALTH INTERESTS

FEMINISTS HAVE A strong history of lobbying for attention to medical concerns specific to women. From the first publication of the widely distributed *Our Bodies, Ourselves*,[1] to the creation of the Office on Women's Health at the National Institutes of Health, advocates have taken the initiative to challenge medical definitions and scientific studies of women's bodies. Now, the topic of women's health has become mainstream enough to warrant media coverage from television news, national and local newspapers, and magazines. When the Congressional Caucus for Women's Interests[2] unveiled its first Women's Health Equity Act in 1990, both Republican and Democratic women joined in efforts to increase funding for breast cancer and other diseases specific to women.[3] The pink ribbon, a symbol made wildly popular by breast cancer advocates, not only represents the need for attention to the issue, but the fact that women's health concerns are no longer relegated to clandestine discussions between friends or those associated only with feminist activists.

That women's health issues cut party lines and cross ideological boundaries is not lost on CWA and IWF. The groups employ a "women's health" frame—a variation on their women's interests frame—when pressing for restrictions on access to abortions (CWA) or when advocating for loosening government control over the production of medical knowledge and technologies (IWF). In recognizing the high priority of women's health issues to lawmakers and the public, the organizations acknowledge the success of feminists but offer alternative, yet gendered, interpretations of these issues.

CWA reaches out to women who are either ambivalent about the legality of abortion or to those who have supported abortion rights but whose opinions are less strongly held. To do so, it takes opposition to abortion, an issue central to social conservatism, and talks about it in terms of women's health interests.

True to its ideological roots, IWF calls for "tort reform" and chastises advocates who push for the regulation of businesses and agencies that center around scientific research and product development. The bases for IWF's claims are free-market beliefs that too much government "interference" stunts productivity and constrains the ability of those in the fields of science and technology to seek innovative solutions. Economic conservatives, like IWF, also argue that overzealous litigation stymies corporations and ultimately hurts their financial bottom lines. To that end, IWF champions legislation aimed at restricting the liability of businesses and limiting damages to plaintiffs. However, IWF couches these matters in terms of women's health, mediated through its economic conservative ideology. Like CWA, IWF shifts the focus of conservative arguments while also redefining women's interests.

CWA AND ABORTION: REACHING OUT TO ABORTION'S "OTHER" VICTIMS

Opposition to abortion and most forms of birth control[4] has been central to CWA's agenda since its inception. CWA lobbies for legislation to put limits on abortion or to make it illegal and opposes federal funding of most domestic and international family-planning programs. Given that the issue is one that lies at the heart of social conservatism, it should be expected that the organization places so much emphasis on these issues. But to encourage a range of women to be sympathetic to its interpretations, CWA has to offer arguments that resonate with a population used to access to reproductive services but who also may feel ambivalent about abortion and its effects on women. Public opinion polls about abortion show that many people favor some restrictions, but most are reluctant to support laws that make the procedure completely illegal.[5] CWA taps into this uncertainty about abortion and challenges the feminist assertion that, when it comes to abortion rights, it is in the interest of women to be prochoice.

While CWA's position on reproductive health issues is consistent with many other social conservative organizations that oppose abortion because of beliefs about fetal "sanctity of life" (e.g., Focus on the Family, National Right to Life Committee, Family Research Council), it also argues that abortion and most forms of contraception hurt women. That is, it shines a spotlight on women's health to signal that opposition to abortion protects women's physical and emotional well-being. Women are, according to CWA, "abortion's second victims."[6] The organization argues that women suffer tremendously from having abortions and those who have them are at greater risk of developing breast cancer than women who have not had abortions. Speaking as women about women's health interests enables CWA to tackle prochoice advocates, who have long argued for attention to women's bodies and lives in reproductive health care debates. Indeed, CWA declared of the prochoice National Abortion and Reproductive Rights Action League that "any campaign that pushes abortion promotes the pain abortion inflicts on women."[7] Invoking women's health needs in these cases neither overrides nor overshadows CWA's concerns about fetal rights. Nor are these narratives antithetical to its religious mission. Instead, they coexist with and expand the boundaries of conservative arguments about abortion.

At its ideological core, CWA's desire to restrict women's reproductive health choices stems from the way its leaders and supporters interpret their religious convictions. That is, the organization construes biblical passages to mean that "God gives life before birth and cares for the unborn."[8] Specifically, it cites the following text from Psalm 139 to champion its determined point of view that fetal life is sacred:

> For You formed my inward parts; You covered me in my mother's womb. I will praise You, for I am fearfully and wonderfully made; Marvelous are Your works, And that my soul knows very well. My frame was not hidden from You, When I was made in secret, And skillfully wrought in the lowest parts of the earth. Your eyes saw my substance, being yet unformed. And in Your book they all were written, The days fashioned for me, When as yet there were none of them.

Despite having some success with this line of reasoning, CWA, along with other self-proclaimed prolife advocates, decided it was important to juxtapose its fetal rights arguments with those pertaining to women's health. Through national and local media appearances, mobilization of its grassroots, antiabortion rallies, and distribution of its publications at churches, it hopes to broaden the appeal of its antiabortion[9] messages, by reaching out to women and men who may not be convinced of the fetal life claims but who may be swayed by arguments that abortions psychologically and physically harm women. In the case of reproductive health, CWA has translated its social conservative arguments into ones more consistent with feminist claims about women's health as it seeks to bring women into conservative causes. This has been a consciously articulated strategy on the part of CWA. In an article posted on its Web site, CWA reveals that it has adopted a plan proposed by antiabortion activist and medical doctor David Reardon. CWA quotes Reardon as arguing, "when pro-abortion advocates understand we are not attacking women, they are more open to communication. Focusing on the woman begins conversation on abortion in the public arena. 'If you help the mother, you help the baby.'"[10]

In following Reardon's logic, CWA contends that its antiabortion proposals should "promote the well being of women. Activists on both sides of abortion should be able to agree on that priority."[11] One way that CWA has implemented this strategy of articulating a "woman's perspective" about abortion policy can be found in its discussions about what it calls "post abortion syndrome" (PAS). Likened to post-traumatic stress disorder, PAS is shorthand for what the organization believes are a litany of negative physical and psychological effects that women face after having abortions. For example:

> Post-abortive women may: require psychological treatment/therapy, suffer post-traumatic stress disorder, experience sexual dysfunction, engage in suicidal thoughts or attempt suicide, become heavy or habitual smokers, abuse alcohol and illegal drugs, acquire eating disorders, neglect or abuse other children, have relationship problems, have repeat abortions, re-experience the abortion through flashbacks, be preoccupied with becoming pregnant to replace the aborted child [and] experience anxiety and guilt.[12]

Some feminists have responded by noting that the "syndrome" is not recognized by any association of medical professionals, nor have researchers been able to demonstrate the level of emotional distress that CWA claims abortion causes.[13] Nonetheless, CWA presses on with this strategy and with its mission of putting women at the center of abortion debates. For example, in conjunction with other antiabortion advocates, like Feminists for Life, it endorses and works with clinics, or "crisis pregnancy centers," that dissuade women from having abortions and counsels them about PAS. Abortion rights advocates, like Planned Parenthood Federation of America (PPFA), oppose these clinics, arguing:

> [They] pose as objective health facilities using neutral-sounding names and deceptive advertising practices that lead women facing unintended pregnancies to believe that they will be offered unbiased counseling and a full range of reproductive health services.... [Instead, they] dissuade women from choosing abortion by subjecting them to inaccurate, anti-choice propaganda and intimidation. Women are exposed to films and written materials that lie about the nature of abortion, the development of the fetus, and the medical and "psychological" effects of abortion. The false information is designed to scare women into carrying pregnancies to term.[14]

For its part, CWA encourages members of Congress to fund these clinics and worked with Representative Joe Pitts (R-PA) in 2004 to hold a hearing on depression after pregnancy before the House Energy and Commerce Subcommittee on Health. During this hearing, two women—one a medical doctor, the other an antiabortion activist— urged Congress to support services for women facing postabortion stress and to consider legislation to fund research on the subject. Although lawmakers did not pass any research bill, they allocated $30 million in federal funds between 2001 and 2005 to support these "crisis pregnancy centers."[15] CWA also refers its constituents and others who come upon its Web site to these services and to organizations like Hope after Abortion (hopeafterabortion.org), a national network of Catholic postabortion counselors. In emphasizing women's responses to abortion, CWA adeptly shifts the focus from its religious discourse about the fetus to one that could resonate with any woman who has had or who may choose to have an abortion. In contrast, although prochoice groups may not deny that having an abortion is difficult for a woman, they often fail to directly address the challenges women face after having the procedure for fear of drawing attention to the downside of the process.

One issue where women have come together across party and ideological lines is breast cancer. From grassroots efforts, to women in Congress, advocates have increased funding for and attention to this disease. CWA is keenly aware of the salience of this issue to women[16] and forcefully argues that abortions can increase women's chances of getting this much-feared cancer. In claiming that "abortion can significantly increase a woman's risk of getting breast cancer," it contends that "abortion is deadly—not only for unborn children, but also for the women who abort them."[17] Its argument is based on a meta-analysis conducted by Brind, Chinchilli, Severs, and Summy-Long.[18] As summarized by CWA, Brind et al. argue:

> [E]arly in her pregnancy, a woman experiences a major surge of estrogen that causes immature breast cells to multiply. These cells are allegedly more susceptible to carcinogens, but are protected when a woman begins to lactate. If her pregnancy is aborted, however, the women's breast cells are left in the vulnerable state, because they do not receive the benefit of lactation that comes from full-term pregnancies.[19]

The prochoice PPFA notes, however, that in an analysis of the approximately twenty-five studies examining the link between breast cancer and abortion, cancer researchers at the National Cancer Institute and the American Cancer Society found no relationship.[20] Similarly, a Harvard study published in April 2007 found no conclusive correlation between abortion and breast cancer.[21] Without acknowledgment of these conclusions, CWA urges lawmakers to require reproductive health professionals to inform women of this alleged association and touts the case of a woman who sued a North Dakota clinic for false advertising when it claimed in a pamphlet that no correlation has been found between abortion and breast cancer.[22] Much to the dismay of CWA, a judge found for the medical provider. However, three states now require doctors to warn women seeking abortions of the alleged link if the doctors determine that scientific evidence warrants the disclaimer.[23] Although CWA has yet to meet with national success on this issue, a 2006 federal government report found that many crisis pregnancy centers counseled young women seeking assistance that abortions cause breast cancer or infertility and urged those who called for help to carry their pregnancies to term.[24] This pattern of activism, that is, using science to support its social conservative causes, is one that other conservative groups have been using for some time. Scholars and critics of right-wing politics note the heightened and sometimes successful use of this tactic, especially with President George W. Bush in office, and argue that it helps to make religious values seem "rational" and bear more weight.[25] CWA's appeal to "science," then, roots it firmly within the broader conservative movement, giving it legitimacy among this population and with like-minded elected officials.

CWA also condemns international family-planning programs that provide women with Norplant. Norplant, introduced in the United States in 1991, is a form of birth control inserted under the skin in "matchstick" form and contains hormones that prevent pregnancies in about 99% of the women who use it. Generally, Norplant works by inhibiting ovulation, therefore preventing women from releasing eggs for fertilization. However, Norplant can also affect hormones that allow a fertilized egg to be implanted in the uterus, and thus CWA considers the drug to be an abortifacient. On these grounds alone, CWA opposes Norplant, but it also frames its opposition in terms of women's health. A number of women have had adverse side effects, such as irregular bleeding, headaches, nausea, dizziness, and depression, from using the drug, which is meant to stay in the body for up to five years. In 1999, American Home Products, Inc., the makers of Norplant, agreed to pay 36,000 users of the contraception about $1,500 each, for failing to adequately warn women about these ill effects. The company never admitted wrongdoing, and several other previous cases against it were dismissed.[26] Because of these potential health concerns and because of reports that some doctors would not remove the birth control when requested due to cost or because they felt that the women needed to have continued contraceptive use,[27] CWA refers to women in the United States and abroad who use Norplant as "human guinea pigs."[28]

CWA is especially focused on ending the supply of Norplant to women in other countries since Norplant was pulled from the market in the United States in 2002, in part due to the many negative side effects women were experiencing. CWA contends that "the U.S. government is using our money to bruise and batter women and children around the world"[29] and lobbies lawmakers to abolish the use of federal funds for any family-planning programs that promote it. For example, it opposes U.S. funding for the international UN Fund for Population Activities (usually referred to as the UN Population Fund; UNFPA), in part because UNFPA counsels women about abortions and also provides them with Norplant and other "abortifacients." Its arguments have been taken seriously by some policymakers: under George W. Bush's administration, the United States has withheld money from UNFPA (over $200 million between 2002 and 2007), arguing that it promotes coercive reproductive health policies. Here, CWA's arguments are reminiscent of feminist critiques about sterilization abuse. Over the years, feminist activists have argued that poor women and women of color have been subjected to discrimination when it comes to the application of reproductive health policies. Some have documented cases where women were sterilized without their knowledge or encouraged by health care professionals to undergo procedures like hysterectomies to impede or eliminate their ability to have more children.[30] Other women's health activists have decried the suggestion of some policymakers that women on welfare be offered free Norplant to stem their child bearing.[31]

By advocating internationally on reproductive health issues and making claims about the potentially harmful health effects on poor women in other countries, CWA constructs itself as an organization that extends its reach widely. As it works with members of Congress to block funding for international family-planning programs, it also helps to counter the claim that conservatives are indifferent to these oft-neglected populations of women. In this case, CWA may give conservatism some legitimacy among the range of activists who call for more attention to economically disadvantaged populations around the world.

Feeling uncertain that *Roe v. Wade* will ever be overturned, antiabortion proponents have engaged in a campaign to restrict some of the most uncommon, yet most disturbing sounding of abortions—late-term ones. CWA and other antiabortion activists have lobbied state and federal lawmakers to outlaw procedures they refer to as "partial birth abortions" or PBA. Known as a "D&X," or dilation and extraction procedure, it requires a fetus to be removed intact from a woman. The process is most common in second- and third-trimester abortions (after twenty-four weeks) and is performed when the fetus's and/or woman's health or life is seriously endangered. According to the PPFA (which cites the Centers for Disease Control), in the United States only 1.5% of all abortions are performed after the first twenty weeks of pregnancy.[32] Nonetheless, on the subject of these third-trimester abortions, CWA writes that not only is the end result of such an abortion a "dead child" but that, for women, the procedure can be dangerous. To this effect it argues: "partial-birth abortion is an invitation to infection and subsequent infertility. Pulling a child feet first out of the mother could seriously injure her or cause her death because the procedure risks tearing her uterus or lacerating the cervix or lower uterine segment."[33]

Although it provides little scientific data to back up this specific contention, it does offer other information to help support its claims. For example, in a report detailing its opposition to PBA, CWA noted that sixteen physicians who testified before Congress about the procedure said it would cause "significant harm to specific women and would materially increase the risk of sterilization, infection, and other serious health consequences."[34] Not all of these doctors opposed the D&X procedure, but they were instead comparing it to a potentially safer, alternative form of abortion that could be used during this stage of the pregnancy. Nevertheless, CWA highlighted the witnesses' health-related claims and used them in lobbying materials and information disseminated to the public to ground their challenges to PBA.

Antiabortion groups like CWA see opposition to this procedure as a way to make some inroads in blocking access to abortions. Indeed, through their advocacy efforts, more than half of the states and the federal government have passed versions of laws banning "partial birth abortions." CWA's state and national efforts included meeting with legislators, encouraging its grassroots to send letters and make phone calls, and supporting nominees to the U.S. Supreme Court who oppose all forms of abortion. Opponents of CWA argue that these anti-PBA laws have been intentionally written in broad terms so that most second-trimester abortions could be banned under these policies.

Whatever the intentions, it appears that CWA's efforts have been rewarded in this case. In 2003, Congress passed and President Bush signed into law the Partial-Birth Abortion Ban Act.[35] This legislation outlaws most forms of third-trimester abortions and contains language claiming that such abortions pose "serious risks to the long-term health of women and in some circumstances, their lives." Several prochoice and civil liberties groups enacted legal challenges to its implementation, but the U.S. Supreme Court upheld the law in 2007,[36] handing antiabortion advocates a major legal victory. During this battle, CWA joined other conservative groups like the Christian Legal Society, Alliance Defense Fund, National Association of Evangelicals, Focus on the Family, and Family Research Council in an amicus brief that was written in support of the Partial-Birth Abortion Ban Act.

Extending its reach beyond surgical abortions, CWA also condemns the abortifacient RU-486, unlicensed abortion clinics, and the contraceptive pill. For example, in a piece entitled "RU-486: Killer Pills," one author warns women of the "dangerous" side effects of RU-486, or Mifepristone, a series of pills taken by women after they learn they are pregnant, should they want to terminate the pregnancy. RU-486 works by blocking progesterone, a hormone necessary to sustain a pregnancy. Although approved for use by the FDA, CWA contends:

> Women who took RU-486 in clinical trials experienced firsthand just how "easy" the abortion pill is. Common side effects included: painful contractions, nausea, vomiting, diarrhea, pelvic pain and spasms, and headaches—as well as the trauma of seeing their aborted baby.... Chemical abortions like RU-486 will not advance women's health.[37]

Consistent with its concerns about RU-486, CWA has lobbied diligently to keep the "morning-after pill" off the market. Morning-after pills, also known as "emergency contraception," contain hormones that can reduce the chances of a woman getting pregnant when started within 120 hours of having unprotected intercourse. It works by preventing ovulation. In the summer of 2006, after intense political fighting over the availability of these drugs, and even some temporary victories for CWA, the Food and Drug Administration approved the availability of "Plan B," or emergency contraception, compelling CWA to write talking points about this turn of events. Its fact sheet begins with the phrase "the morning-after pill (MAP) lacks testing for safety to women." It goes on to detail myriad "potential risks to women" but never mentions the destruction of fetal life among its critiques of the pharmaceutical.[38] Instead, it focuses on women's physical and emotional health concerns. Similarly, in a pamphlet detailing the negative side effects of most forms of "high-tech" birth control, CWA rhetorically asks women if contraceptives are "health care" or a "health risk." In the same brochure, it also cautions women: "In the past 35 years, various chemicals and devices that manipulate women's reproductive systems have come on the medical scene. Women need to know precisely what they do and what risks they present."[39]

Such cautionary rhetoric is not far from feminist critiques of the medical establishment for encouraging women to take medications or hormones or use birth control like Depo-Provera, which some women's health advocates claim have not been fully tested or proven relatively harmless. And with this line of reasoning, feminists have had some success in making policymakers and the general public amenable to their position. When CWA invokes a similar set of arguments, it helps the conservative movement appear to be in sync with a range of political activists and thus has the potential to widen CWA's appeal and construct the organization as science savvy as well. Clearly, its reproductive health narratives further CWA's social conservative antiabortion stance. Of course, this is intentional on the part of CWA. Since feminists have long argued for redirecting attention from fetal rights to women's health concerns in abortion debates,[40] using women's interests frames enables the organization to counter feminist claims that the legality of abortion promotes women's well-being. However, CWA also demonstrates how a group of conservative women can be antiabortion and do so from a "woman's perspective." This provides CWA some status as a women's organization and helps other conservatives claim that their movement cares about women and their health.

Like CWA, IWF uses the language of women's health to articulate conservative views on some of its policy issues. Unlike CWA, IWF does not take an official position on abortion because many economic conservatives believe that government should not be involved in these debates. It prefers to welcome women with a range of views on the subject. That both organizations prioritize women's health in some form, however, is a nod to the influence of feminist activism and the need for these conservative women's groups to respond to issues that feminists have defined for legislators and the public.

As part of its health policy platform, IWF contends that there is too much government intervention into medical and scientific research and that "politics" has undermined objectivity in research. *Politics*, in this case, refers to the activism of liberal environmental, public health, and/or feminist organizations. IWF's reasoning emanates from economic principles that call for less regulation of businesses, including those related to the production of pharmaceuticals and medical technologies, and from its belief that civil litigation against the health industry needs to be reined in by tort reform. IWF is also critical of the precautionary principle. According to supporters of this point of view, the *precautionary principle* is

> when an activity raises threats of harm to human health or the environment, precautionary measures should be taken even if some cause and effect relationships are not fully established scientifically. In this context the proponent of an activity, rather than the public, should bear the burden of proof. The process of applying the precautionary principle must be open, informed and democratic and must include potentially affected parties. It must also involve an examination of the full range of alternatives, including no action.[41]

Many environmental, public health, and feminist women's health advocates encourage adopting these values. Like feminists who lobbied for protective labor legislation on the grounds that such policies protected employees, the precautionary principle is seen as a way to make businesses accountable and responsive to consumers. Economic conservatives, including IWF, however, are critical of the precautionary principle, which fellow conservatives from the American Enterprise Institute refer to as "paralyzing" and indicative of an "obsessive fear of the unknown."[42] These conservative groups believe that such trepidation negatively affects businesses by allowing for government regulations that can slow down research, product development, and financial growth.

Given IWF's belief in free-market values, it makes sense that it opposes rules perceived to interfere with business and scientific practices. But IWF is not just another conservative organization lobbying against laws that conform to the precautionary principle. It is also a women's group that claims that such norms differentially harm and affect women. That is, it brings a gendered perspective to these debates, encouraging its allies and the public to view these issues through a different lens. IWF has held conferences and briefings, sponsored health fellows, written numerous press releases, and, for a time, published a "Weird Science Watch." All of these efforts are meant to call attention to the ways in which "dubious science," such as claims that silicone breast implants cause irreparable damage or that using nail polish is dangerous to women's health, "harms women."[43] As with the other issues discussed in this book, IWF offers a unique addition to the conservative movement with regard to debates about the precautionary principle, tort reform, and government funding of research. Like CWA, which reconceptualizes conservative views about abortion from the perspective of women's bodies, IWF claims that attacks on science and health research and industries must be considered in light of their implications for women.

THE GENDERED DYNAMICS OF HEALTH AND SCIENCE POLICY

How does IWF shape economic conservative positions on scientific research and enterprises to be consistent with women's interests? How are its narratives different from those of feminists, who have long argued that women's health issues must be prioritized? What, in the case of IWF, are women's health concerns?

Feminist women's health efforts are premised on the notion that women's bodies are biologically different from men's and that research should include adequate attention to these distinctions. In addition, many feminists have argued that male doctors are prone to making sexist assumptions about women's emotional and physical well-being, and some of them fail to really take seriously symptoms that women articulate. Feminist women's health organizations, like National Women's Health Network, support the precautionary principle on the grounds that "evidence, rather than profit, should drive the services offered and information that is made available to women."[44]

As noted, many feminist views about women's health have been accepted widely enough to increase government funding for diseases like breast and cervical cancer, and their efforts have made these issues of concern to a bipartisan group of lawmakers, advocates, and the general public. As Debra Dodson documents, starting in the late 1980s, the Congressional Caucus for Women's Issues (CCWI), which is a bipartisan group of women in Congress, worked along with women's health activists and supportive men in the House and Senate to push for the enactment of the Women's Health Equity Act (WHEA). WHEA came on the heels of public hearings held by Representative Henry Waxman (D-CA) that revealed that the NIH was not complying with its own standards for including women in clinical trials. Women's health advocates argued that omitting women from this research was dangerous as it meant that medical professionals and patients would have limited information about how drugs and procedures specifically affect women. The well-publicized hearings drew public outrage and opened a window of opportunity for women lawmakers to join across party lines and push for a range of women's health concerns. These included research and services related to breast cancer, contraception, AIDS, osteoporosis, infant mortality, and cervical cancer.[45] The outcomes of these efforts were increases in funding for and attention to women's health issues. For example, in 1981 the National Cancer Institute, an agency within NIH, spent $33.9 million on breast cancer research. By 1998, that grew to $348.2 million, a tenfold increase. In addition, breast cancer receives more federal funding than any other prevalent cancer, including lung, prostate, and colorectal.[46] Women's advocacy also led to the creation of the Office of Women's Health (OWH) within the U.S. Department of Health and Human Services, representing a commitment at the national level to attention to women's health concerns. With OWH in place, the federal government now has centralized women's health activities. Specifically, OWH

> coordinates the efforts of all the HHS agencies and offices involved in women's health and works to improve the health and well-being of women and girls in the United States through its innovative programs, by educating health professionals, and motivating behavior change in consumers through the dissemination of health information.[47]

Seeking to be taken seriously as an organization that represents women, IWF cannot lightly dismiss how successful feminists have been at institutionalizing their efforts. Indeed, it is risky for IWF to challenge feminists on this topic. Nonetheless, IWF believes that feminists have exaggerated the extent to which women are discriminated against by doctors and taken advantage of by researchers in order to promote a feminist agenda and get more research money from the federal government. It also contends that feminist advocacy causes women to be unnecessarily fearful, cautious, and skeptical. IWF hopes that its framing of these issues in terms of women's interests from an economic conservative point of view will move people to question feminist assessments and actions.

For IWF, attention to women's health interests rests on certain assumptions about women's needs and behaviors. It argues that women are more risk averse than men and thus less willing to allow for scientific "innovation" and the testing and marketing of new treatments. That is, according to IWF, women are more prone to support the precautionary principle, an inclination it sees as harmful. IWF's rationale for sponsoring a conference on "junk science" exemplifies this point of view. According to IWF, *junk science* is science motivated by politics, which lacks solid empirical findings and may disproportionately affect women:

> Those of us who follow the junk science debate know that scientific illiteracy is certainly not gender-specific. But survey data—such as compiled in 1996 by the Harvard Center for Risk Analysis—do show that women, as a group, tend to be more risk-averse. That's why the IWF has chosen to explore the relationship between unjustified fears and health and science policy.[48]

IWF contends that women are more likely than men to believe warnings about potential public health dangers, even if, according to the organization, the conclusions are neither solid nor indisputable. It also argues that, since women make the majority of health care decisions for families, they are disproportionately affected by science and health care policies. As such, how women process information and make these decisions are critical topics for a women's organization to tackle. For example, in arguing that women's health and other liberal advocates are trying to get women to blindly accept feminist critiques about medical research, one IWF leader notes:

> The problem is a lot of the way government policy is currently produced; actual research is not available for public consumption. So women by the way tend to play the role of almost the top health care advisor for their families. We internalize a lot of concerns, we choose the doctors, in many instances we pay the bills. We have a more sensitized

risk component to us, meaning [if] someone says there is a 1 in 1,000 chance or 1 in 18,000 chance that your child is going to be hurt by this, we tend to project our children into that role. We are much more sensitive to risk. What I believe has happened is that women's fears are often falsely manipulated to further an agenda. I am fine with us being [aware, but] I mean, I can't be scared of everything. I have five kids and a job, tell me what I should be scared of? ... [W]hen we started peeling back the layers of what made it difficult to compare relative risks, it was the lack of transparency in government, the lack of access to data, the lack of the ability to replicate epidemiological analyses. I like peer review, I am a very simple person. ... We can't walk around being scared of everything all the time. It is first of all not accurate, and we have to make the right decisions for our families. And stop telling us we are stupid and you can inform us. Just give us the information.[49]

By claiming that women are more risk averse and in charge of family health care needs, IWF articulates why women have a special stake in science and health policy. And its gendered analysis of these issues is promoted in several ways. First, as part of its annual "Agenda for Women" report, which is distributed to IWF members, lawmakers, and the public, IWF includes sections explaining why "women should care" about how research studies are conducted, reported, and funded. Specifically, it states that, for women to make "sound decisions" about their and their families' health care needs, they need clear and adequate explanations of the conclusions offered by researchers. To this end, it argues for the release of raw data to the public so that others may analyze the information and urges those who report on studies related to issues like environmental health risks to more adequately put those risks into context. This, according to IWF, will help women who are "concerned about the complicated and often conflicting news and advice that is meted out each day."[50] Second, IWF aims to "debunk" what it considers to be health scares about a number of women's medical issues, such as silicone breast implants and autoimmune disease, pesticides and decreased sperm counts, dioxin and birth defects, and tampons and reproductive tract problems. It prides itself on revealing "the lack of evidence to support any of these claims" and charges that such allegations only bring on expensive lawsuits and needless government regulations, while limiting the availability of new medical products and treatments.[51] For example, injecting itself into the highly publicized and controversial debate over the safety of breast implants, IWF asserts that, since women are more cautious, they are more easily duped into believing feminist health advocates' claims that implants cause grave health dangers. IWF warns that women should not be so easily led into fearing the effects of implants and urges women to make decisions about the procedure free from undue influence. To this end, one prominent IWF leader related this to me:

> I read five newspapers every day, read magazines. And the breast implant scare was really big then. And I had read every woman's magazine article on breast implants, and how it was terrible, these women were misled into it. And the healthy kind of underlying theme of: why were they having them anyway? Again, I am big on, if they wanted to have them, why do you care? Isn't this their decision? But the science showed that there was a greater risk [from] the general anesthetic procedures than there was to any breast implant. As an analytic type, this was so at odds with what I was reading and hearing on the news, so I was like, this can't be true. So I go back and tell all sorts of scientists they must be lying because after all everyone knows....And they started walking me through the actual science of it. And I kind of lost my innocence there, I am like, oh my gosh, this has been completely misportrayed to the American public. And worse than that, the fear, the scare, all these women who had breast implants were running back to have them taken out.[52]

Like the case of breast implants, there are many instances in which companies are sued when their products produce negative health effects. IWF contends that such litigation stymies research and comes at the expense of business productivity and profitability. It considers these outcomes to be related to aggressive adherence to the precautionary principle. To counteract what it sees as negative implications of the precautionary principle, it supports legislative efforts toward "tort reform."[53] For IWF, *tort reform* refers to limiting or restricting litigation and damage awards in cases involving medical malpractice and other lawsuits. Those invoking the term *tort reform* generally believe that businesses are unduly harmed when judges and juries liberally allow plaintiffs the right to sue and/or determine they are eligible for large sums of money when they win cases against the defendants. IWF connects its concerns about tort reform and the well-being of businesses to women's health by equating attacks on business with injury to women. According to IWF:

> Given the huge amounts of money that are at stake in the typical mass lawsuit, it's no wonder American companies are reluctant to develop

new contraceptive products. What rational business planner wouldn't prefer to concentrate on lipstick and deodorant? The result for American women, however, is that they have access to fewer methods of birth control than women in the rest of the developed world.[54]

In addition, IWF asserts that feminist attempts to hold businesses responsible for injuries to women have backfired. In 1996, for example, some conservative members of Congress tried to pass the Common Sense Product Liability Legal Reform Act. The bill would have capped punitive damages for consumers at $250,000 or twice the economic damages and would have eliminated punitive damages altogether for products that had obtained premarket approval from the FDA. When President Clinton and feminist organizations opposed the bill (which passed both chambers of Congress), IWF charged that the unintended consequence of their opposition would be fewer birth control options for women. Here, IWF links its implicit support for birth control to economic conservative issues and ultimately frames tort reform as a women's health issue. That is, if businesses that sold contraceptives did not fear being sued if a product proved to be harmful to some women, those companies would be more willing to put resources into developing new forms of family planning. Under President George W. Bush's tenure, the issue of tort reform arose again, this time with a president who supported caps on damages. In 2003, Bush issued a call for limiting the amount of money that juries can award to victims of medical malpractice, claiming that such cases greatly increase insurance premiums for businesses, families, and individuals. Although Congress has yet to pass specific legislation to address Bush's concerns,[55] IWF praised the president for helping women by calling attention to the gendered nature of small business ownership and family medical decisions:

> Women are especially being harmed by this economic drag on medicine. Far too many small business owners find the cost of health insurance prohibitive, and women own the majority of new small businesses. More and more female heads of household can't afford insurance at all. And skyrocketing malpractice insurance costs are driving many doctors out of obstetrics and gynecology, for example. When the President speaks of a woman having to live with family in another state because no ob-gyn could take her case in her hometown, he's only illustrating an extreme case of a real life problem faced by women nationwide. IWF has long called for meaningful tort reform that, among other things, would increase penalties for frivolous lawsuits, curb the use of "junk

science" in courtroom testimony, and restrict overreaching actions by judges and juries.[56]

By taking the side of women who want implants, or "revealing" the problems with strict regulation of the development of drugs, IWF considers itself to be a resource for women who want the "truth." To counteract feminists and get its message out, it publicizes its views on national television and radio, holds informational sessions for legislators and their staffs, and offers reports and documents to its members. In addition, this theme of debunking health and science beliefs was carried out by IWF when it denounced so-called myths perpetuated by feminist professors in the ad it placed in university newspapers.[57] In that highly charged challenge to scholars and educators, IWF claimed that the notion expressed by feminists that "women have been short-changed in medical research" is unfounded and that it is espoused by educators, health care activists, and members of Congress only to advance feminism. IWF was referring specifically to actions (discussed above) taken by the CCWI and women's health advocates against NIH for not adequately including women as subjects in clinical trials and avoiding research on diseases unique to women, despite being directed to do so by Congress. As I already noted, the outcome of these efforts was a significant increase in funding for research on diseases like breast cancer and better enforcement of NIH's policy to include women in its studies. Even many conservative women in Congress were on board with this initiative. However, in the newspaper ad, IWF blasted these advocates by claiming that they were led by "gender feminists" looking for "power struggles within the medical profession."[58] The derogatory term *gender feminists* is taken from the work of IWF national advisory board member Christina Hoff Sommers. Sommers says that gender feminists believe that all of our institutions, "from the state to the family to the grade schools, perpetuate male dominance" and that women "are virtually under siege." As such, gender feminists "seek vindication and ammunition,"[59] and in this case, according to IWF, their target is a medical community designed to promote patriarchy and oppress women. In framing women's health advocacy in ways that suggest fraudulence, self-interest, and radicalism, IWF sets itself up as an organization that is reasonable and rational. In this way, it seeks to convince women of its claim that feminists have a strong hold on government resources and are using them to promote an extremist and misguided agenda. While its messages in this case may not be popular with everyone, that it speaks as a women's organization to lawmakers and the public may cause these audiences to reconsider the meaning of women's interests and whether or not women are really being well served by women's health policies as promoted by feminists.

As part of its campaign to cast economic conservative values in terms of women's interests, IWF also criticizes the process by which public health studies are conducted. Feminists have long charged that biases taint science,[60] but have concluded that objectivity may not be a possibility. Although feminist scientists and scholars have not come to a singular conclusion over how to eliminate or address subjectivity in research, generally they start from the supposition that biases stem from sexist and racist norms that influence what gets studied, who gets funded, and what is considered appropriate knowledge. In essence, they are making epistemological claims about power and knowledge production.

IWF offers a different assessment, claiming that science can be relatively pure when free from the scrutiny of interest groups and government regulators. The organization argues that studies might fail to use appropriate data sources, but that most people do not know if this is the case. To address these concerns, it urges lawmakers to require researchers to make their data available to the public and explicitly to clarify how their conclusions are drawn. Like its criticism of feminists for allegedly overhyping the incidence of domestic violence, IWF implies that women would calculate their health risks differently if they knew more about how data were collected and evaluated. For example, it argues that, since public health risk assessments made by government officials are premised upon review of existing studies, these officials may intentionally omit results that do not support the conclusions that they believe are in the best interests of the public. In other words, if lawmakers are convinced, either by research and/or by activists, that toxins in tampons hurt women, they will only reference the research that backs up this conclusion and fail to acknowledge any studies that do not. IWF is vague on which issues this may influence, but does suggest that women are more prone to fearing the stated risks than are men. This is not specifically a concern for economic conservatives: many women argue for more accurate depictions of research by the media and urge consumers to be more informed. But IWF suggests that faulty methodology, misinterpretation, and skewed presentations of data are politically motivated and stem from interest groups having too much say in the design and dissemination of research. Without specifying exactly to which studies it is referring, IWF argues that peer review processes, for example, are not applied evenly and that "peer reviewers are often selected for their sympathy toward the study's results."[61] Of course, its criticisms are saved for groups it considers to be "liberal," like feminist and environmental ones. For example, while it does not take a stand on the legality of abortion, it has bemoaned that the public cannot get accurate statistics and information about the relationship between abortion and breast cancer. As noted earlier, these studies have become the center of a political football match. IWF claims that the inability to get this information stems from political pressures that work against "objective research,"[62] or research that is immune from input by advocates. Since IWF does not take a position on reproductive health issues, it does not need to convince its constituents of the need to overturn laws and court rulings that make abortions legal. Nonetheless, it does use the debate over the issue itself to promote its contention that ideology and "politics" impair the research process.

CONCLUSIONS

Social conservatives expend significant amounts of time, money, and energy in trying to make abortion illegal. Indeed, opposition to abortion helped to galvanize activism-shy conservative evangelicals in the late 1970s and ignited a movement that is still strong today.[63] CWA has played a key role in this part of the conservative movement since its formation. Nonetheless, the organization has not, until recently, used its status as a women's organization to promote the idea that it is in the interest of women to be antiabortion. Since many women feel uncertain about abortion and the degree to which it should be available,[64] CWA's framing of reproductive issues can have real effects in terms of public opinion and policy outcomes. That abortions may cause posttraumatic stress disorder or breast cancer can certainly convince some women to move from ambivalence to opposition. It also reshapes the debate about abortion politics, suggesting that social conservative views go beyond concern for the fetus. As feminists and others have criticized groups like CWA for not caring about women (or even children after they are born),[65] rhetoric that concentrates on women's health helps the organization to challenge these attacks.

For IWF, the issue of women's health is tightly linked to its conservative views about free-market economies and decreased regulation of business practices and outcomes. Like CWA, its arguments situate the organization firmly within its conservative realm, while at the same time attending to issues about which a broad range of women care. There are no other national conservative organizations calling on women to take up the cause of tort reform for their own good. As with its other policy goals, IWF provides a way for economic conservatism to appeal directly to women without losing the soul of its ideological views.

Both organizations recognize the salience of women's health to women voters, their constituents, and the general public. And each is well aware of the role that feminist groups have played in making women's health issues into a national priority. By incorporating women's health frames into their repertoires, the groups attend to the conflicting pressures they face as both conservative and women's organizations, and they have met with success in some cases.

Chapter 7

THE POLITICAL IMPLICATIONS OF CONSERVATIVE WOMEN'S ACTIVISM

The similarities and differences between CWA and IWF have been clearly exhibited in this book. Both are conservative women's organizations operating in political contexts in which they must contend with competing values and constituencies, most notably other conservative allies, members, potential members, feminists, the media, and policymakers. Given this environment, each must acknowledge feminist achievements, while simultaneously engaging in strategies that allow them to explicitly chastise feminists for going too far, becoming too radical, and allowing women to believe that they are victims of male power. To do so, they use frames that transform the meaning of feminist issues and values into ones that resonate more closely with conservatives. The construction of their political concerns in terms of women's interests also helps to firmly situate CWA and IWF within the realm of groups that represent women. As is true for other interest groups, framing strategies are essential, and in these particular cases we see how unique political circumstances factor into how the organizations present themselves and the policies they care about.[1]

Because of the variance in their conservative ideologies, their particular policy agendas and specific constituencies are different, but, as I have shown, there is some overlap on the issues for which they advocate. For example, as we saw in chapter 5, both are opposed to most forms of government-funded child care. These similarities make the groups likely candidates for coalition partners, yet they rarely work together. The most notable reason for this is CWA's religiosity. Between its conservative Christian theology and its willingness to support government implementation of things like prayer in school, its evangelical roots are an affront to many of those who lead IWF. As an organization committed to individualism and freedom of choice, the specter of government-supported religion can be quite offensive to IWF's leaders and members. But politics does not preclude disparate groups from forming political partnerships, and both organizations are well aware that the conservative movement has gained from factions putting aside their disagreements in order to work together. Some have attributed the rise of conservatism and the Republican Party to this willingness to operate under such a big tent.[2] As Bernice Reagon reminds us and as many political partnerships have shown us, "coalition work is not work done in your home.... You shouldn't look for comfort."[3] Since both groups are trying to show the limits of feminism and to offer alternative meanings about women's identities and issues, reaching beyond their comfort levels could prove to be quite effective. By making political claims about a range of conservative women, they could show the breadth of their support among conservatives and the potential for women to work together in this movement. The exhibition of coherence and unity among activists suggests to policymakers and the public that these women could be a force with which to reckon.

Another important difference between the two organizations is that IWF projects a less ideologically consistent image than does CWA. CWA believes strongly in a female essence that connects women, renders them different from men, and correlates specifically with women's expressed interests and needs. That is, it is comfortably and proudly essentialist and, as a conservative women's organization, invokes these beliefs to contest feminist values and to align feminist-inspired messages with its own conservative views. As such, forming into a women's organization and making claims as and for women mesh well with its views on gender differences and women's interests.

Conversely, IWF simultaneously criticizes identity politics and gender-based "merit" claims, but acts as women, promotes women's issues, and makes sweeping claims about women's differences from men. In so doing, it not only comes across as an organization prone to contradictions, it vividly exemplifies a problem central to identity politics. That is, it argues that, as a women's organization formed to fight feminists, it must act as women and in the collective interests of women. Although IWF justifies its actions as strategic, it produces meanings about women's identities and policy goals, something it criticizes feminists for doing. These moments of paradox, however, do not really do significant damage to IWF. As I have demonstrated in this book, the organization uses frames that help to make sense of its contradictions and positions itself as an alternative to feminism. And it still gets significant media attention, has access to policymakers, and remains a stable institution. Tempting as it may be for feminists to dismiss IWF, it would make more sense for them to pay close attention to the strategies, goals, and actions of this dynamic and burgeoning political institution.

CWA AND IWF SHAPE THE CONSERVATIVE MOVEMENT

This book has explored how conservative ideology mediates the actions of women's groups. As organizations seeking credibility among other actors in the conservative movement, the work of CWA and IWF is generally consistent with their ideological counterparts. On a more practical level, these organizations must also appeal to conservative donors and policymakers to maintain themselves and to have political influence. As I have demonstrated, as women's organizations that have to attend to both feminist successes and conservative constituencies, paradoxical outcomes may occur. Overall, though, both organizations have weathered critiques and have established themselves as forceful and competent conservative advocates. Indeed, the presence of CWA and IWF gives all conservative movement activists more legitimacy when clashing with feminists and other liberals over the meaning of women's interests.

Their relationship with the conservative movement, however, is not unidirectional. As I have discussed throughout the book, the organizations bridge women to other conservative causes, forging important political alignments and ideological partnerships that broaden and strengthen the appeal of conservative political activism. This is one way that CWA and IWF help to shape the agenda of the conservative movement. There is another component to conservative women's political advocacy that also bears on and complicates our understanding of conservative politics. As women's organizations making political claims, CWA's and IWF's activism disrupts the (mostly) conservative notion that gender differences should be the necessary foundation for a public-private dichotomy in our social and political lives—that is, that women generally belong in the home and men in the public sphere (e.g., paid employment and politics). As I noted in chapter 5, both organizations encourage their members and their publics to translate maternal roles into political ones. Some have criticized CWA for acting politically while they advocate for women to be homemakers.[4] CWA justifies itself by arguing that it is women's moral obligation as wives and mothers to fight for and protect their families. By urging women to act for their families, both groups produce images of mothers that disrupt the notion that motherhood is a private role. Indeed, their activism is seen as a mission of sorts for CWA, which encourages women to be advocates and teaches them "how to lobby from [their] homes."[5] CWA founder LaHaye proudly proclaims of her organization's members:

> They are actively working at the local, state and national levels to derail legislation and education that will harm their families. They are concerned about protecting the rights of families rather than their own personal rights.... They are seeking to fill a concrete need: preserving the nuclear family and society from destruction.[6]

In so doing, CWA justifies its political participation to secure the "rights associated with their obligations"[7] as wives and mothers and brings these issues into the public realm of political life. CWA and IWF reveal the interconnectedness between the private and public— or, really, the boundary's instability—blurring the division while reinforcing it through a call for women to spend more time out of the paid workforce. Nonetheless, neither claims that stay-at-home mothering is inconsistent with activism. As feminists have argued for decades, these conservative women's organizations demonstrate that the personal truly is political.

By obfuscating the line between the private and public, CWA and IWF could also have the effect of encouraging conservative male leaders to locate more women in positions of political and social power. Thus, while many conservatives, especially social conservatives, have longed for a return to traditional gender roles and have fought politically to make this happen, they continue to simultaneously embrace the political participation of women. They are well aware that doing so could help to decrease electoral gender gaps for Republicans, as well as cultivate more women-friendly explanations of conservative goals. In addition, although economic conservatives are generally hostile to identity-based political claims, IWF's prominence as a women's organization gives this type of political organizing legitimacy among that wing of the conservative movement. As such, IWF complicates the meaning of liberal individualism, showing that, within economic conservatism, there is room for identity politics and, perhaps more realistically, the necessity for it.

My research has also demonstrated the importance of using gender as an analytic category to understand fusionism within the conservative movement. Chapter 5 discussed the implications for conservatism when CWA and IWF present similar views about mothering and child care. But it also suggested that scholars need to further explore the places where conservatives will not or cannot work together. We know from this study and other research that religiosity can divide these activists—but so too can other beliefs about women and the role of government. As I discussed in chapter 4, CWA is more likely to view government as a means to reducing the availability and effects of pornography. Conversely, IWF is much more skeptical about the function of the state when it comes to developing public policies that address violence against women. Thus, we see that fusionism among conservatives can be hindered by perceptions of women's roles vis-à-vis the state.

On the other hand, since neither group, especially IWF, is immune from compromising its core values for political expediency (which is, of course, true for many interest groups), there will be times when the organizations can mobilize conservatives who are not their members to work on certain issues. For example, CWA and IWF both oppose gender-integrated basic training in the military; leaders from IWF and CWA even shared a podium at a press conference on the issue. The organizations also condemn affirmative action policies and together have criticized the international Platform for Action. The platform was conceived at the 1995 Fourth World Conference on Women in Beijing, where government officials and activists from around the world gathered to produce a collaborative statement that advocates could take back to their home countries and use in their push for women's rights. Specifically, the document calls for "women's empowerment" and framing women's rights as human rights. It urges governments, the international community, nongovernmental organizations, and the private sector to address issues like women's poverty, unequal access to education and training, inequalities in access to health care, violence against women, and the inadequate promotion and protection of the human rights of women.[8] CWA and IWF oppose the platform and the role of international intervention in this case on the grounds that it raises serious sovereignty issues by "putting enormous power over federal and state domestic law into the hands of a United Nations committee."[9] They also contend that the statement promotes a narrow, and predominantly feminist, view of women's interests. CWA bemoans, for example, that through the process of developing the platform, "feminists [in the United States] are using the United Nations to force their agenda on other nations."[10] It also raises concerns that the document calls for safe and legal access to abortions and fails to condemn homosexuality.

Similarly, both oppose the United States' ratification of the Convention on the Elimination of All Forms of Discrimination against Women (CEDAW), which IWF claims is a "project of the feminist Left...that undermines national sovereignty."[11] CEDAW was adopted in 1979 by the UN General Assembly and is often described as an international bill of rights for women. The document defines what constitutes discrimination against women and sets up an agenda for national action to end women's oppression. Specifically, CEDAW defines discrimination against women as

> any distinction, exclusion or restriction made on the basis of sex which has the effect or purpose of impairing or nullifying the recognition, enjoyment or exercise by women, irrespective of their marital status, on a basis of equality of men and women, of human rights and fundamental freedoms in the political, economic, social, cultural, civil or any other field.[12]

Countries that have ratified or acceded to CEDAW are legally bound to put its provisions into practice and to submit national reports every four years detailing compliance. To date, the United States is among only 8 countries[13] that have not approved the treaty (185 countries have ratified it).

In 2001, CWA and IWF teamed up with other conservative women and held a press conference, organized by CWA, in support of Senator John Ashcroft's nomination to be attorney general. When working for Ashcroft's ultimately successful nomination, both organizations chastised liberals for opposing him, with IWF touting his honesty and CWA arguing that he would "defend the values that made America great."[14] The organizations stood together again in 2005, when they worked with an ad hoc group of conservative women to speak out in favor of

John Roberts's nomination to the U.S. Supreme Court. Conservative women's views prevailed in this case as well. Given these important moments of collaboration, if both organizations choose to put aside their differences, their working together could produce wide-reaching and powerful effects.

Understanding CWA and IWF has implications for evaluating other identity-based conservative organizations, especially those organized around the issue of race. While their numbers are small, there do exist some national conservative organizations that center around racial concerns.[15] For example, Center for Equal Opportunity (CEO), led by former director of the U.S. Commission on Civil Rights Linda Chavez, is "devoted exclusively to the promotion of colorblind equal opportunity and racial harmony."[16] CEO takes conservative positions on issues of affirmative action, immigration, and bilingual education and has worked with IWF. While there are other organizations that hold similar positions, these groups specifically seek to represent and organize people of color to support their conservative positions. As we have seen in this study of CWA and IWF, groups seeking to represent a particular community, like women, Latinos, or black conservatives, must convince lawmakers and the public that they really represent the identity group for which they claim to speak. That is, they bear a unique burden, one that differs from their white conservative counterparts. For example, in opposing affirmative action, the predominantly white, conservative Heritage Foundation might frame its message differently than a group of conservative African Americans claiming to speak on behalf of people from that racial community. Lack of attention to this phenomenon leaves us with incomplete explanations for why conservative organizations act as they do. This study of conservative women's organizations sheds some light on the tactics that matter to groups making identity-based claims and argues for careful attention to the competing influences that shape organizational actions.

THE POLITICS OF IDENTITY: LESSONS FROM CWA AND IWF

As discussed in chapter 3, some feminists have criticized identity politics because of its potential for obscuring differences among women. Butler points out that, when feminist groups make claims as women, they essentialize what it means to be a woman, thus suggesting a homogeneity that does not exist.[17] As I have shown throughout this study, when conservative women's organizations make claims as women about women, they are doing so to counter feminist claims, promote conservative causes, and appeal to a broad range of women. Because these identity-based organizations exist in the same political milieu as feminists, their effects can be simultaneously tempered and profound.

For CWA and IWF, acting as women gives them the legitimacy to counter feminist representational claims. In this way, for them, identity politics is a positive form of political engagement. The relative value of identity-based activism for these groups also points to the salience of gender identity in politics, an outcome made possible by feminist activism. Although their claims exist in the same intellectual and political marketplace as those of feminists, conservative women's constructions can alter our ideas about women, mothers, housewives, and even political activists, depending upon the support they get from policymakers, the public, and the media. This study points to the real and significant consequences of having conservative women's voices reverberating through legislatures and in the media. The presence of CWA and IWF means clashes will occur among women about the meaning of women's status in politics and the family, the nature and origins of gender differences, and the role of government in women's lives. As gender-conscious political institutions, both feminist and conservative women's organizations battle over whose stories about women are most representative. And given that these narratives about women's lives have policy implications, the battle over their authenticity is quite significant. Shane Phelan suggests that "[r]ather than arguing with one another about which story is true, [we] must look instead at what is at stake in our different stories; we must examine the consequences of our stories in terms of power and change."[18]

While CWA and IWF challenge our understanding of women's interests and identities, they also reify the problem of essentialism, which, in this case, is a product of identity-based activism. Through their narratives, CWA and IWF produce what it means to be a woman, a conservative woman, and a mother, based on their values and ideologies about gender roles. For example, their images of the good mother tend to assume that she is married, middle class, and eager to forgo her career. When CWA and IWF invoke gender identity, whether to contest feminists or to transform the meaning of women's issues and interests, they suggest a homogeneity of interests and experiences that does not exist even among conservative women. As channeled through identity-based political organizations, then, the activism of conservative women can suffer from the same weaknesses that feminist groups encounter when they claim to speak for women. This is precisely the concern that IWF cofounder Anita Blair pointed to in chapter 3, as she related why she and other IWF associates feel conflicted about organizing as women. Attention to this dilemma requires that each side needs to be more specific in its claims about women's interests, or they all will continue to be targets for each other as they exploit women's uncertainties about gender roles and other material conflicts to show that they are better able to speak to and for women. While I do not believe we should abandon identity politics—it gives women a sense that their political claims are legitimate and has generated attention from policymakers and the press—the risks of such political engagement require that groups be more specific in their interest-based claims.

My analysis of identity politics and the relevance of gender identity to conservative women's organizations also generates important strategic lessons for feminists by revealing the successes and limits of feminist theory, activism, and identity politics. As I have explained in this book, both CWA and IWF adopt feminist representational strategies by acting collectively as women, promoting women's issues, and framing issues in terms of women's interests. In her study of two antifeminist women's organizations, Susan Marshall[19] also finds that conservative women's organizations have shifted to what she calls a "woman-centered" framing approach, reflecting a co-optation of feminist rhetoric by the groups under study.[20] Marshall contends, rightfully so, that this reflects the success of feminists in making gender salient in the policymaking process and in changing social values about women's roles in the family and workplace. That the women's organizations in my study are concerned with such issues as domestic violence, pornography, and women's health marks a significant gain by feminists, who have long argued for political attention to these issues. Thus, while CWA's and IWF's activism poses a challenge to feminists and identity politics, it also illuminates the fact that conservative politics, political representation, and policy advocacy cannot be fully understood without attention to the role of gender and the feminist movement.

REPRESENTATION AND POLITICAL LEGITIMACY

CWA and IWF have policy agendas consistent with many other conservative organizations. But, as women's organizations that take seriously the connection between gender identity and political strategy, they offer something more than energy and resources to the conservative movement. They offer women—both members and those not yet affiliated with their groups—a chance for political representation. By examining conservative interest groups, we see how the question of representation comes up not only in studying elected officials,[21] but in other contexts as well.

We should diversify how we think about and study political representation to determine what factors may or may not enhance a particular group's feelings of legitimacy and political efficacy. We need to look beyond outcomes and beyond whether or not people are being represented and explore whether or not they feel like they have a stake in the process via their representation by interest groups and other activists. Organized interests have been critiqued for being elitist and narrow,[22] but many women may feel more connected to politics and can be mobilized to participate if they relate to the women making public claims on their behalf. Therefore, we should ask if the presence of women advocates compels citizens to be more politically involved and/or to have more faith in government. Elected women officials believe this to be true,[23] but it has yet to be determined if the mass public feels the same way. Nonetheless, CWA and IWF leaders argue, and I believe rightly, that feeling represented will motivate women to support them and to act politically. Certainly, these are important considerations in a representative democracy. Evaluating the actions of interest groups adds a dynamic component to the assessment of representation. We can also learn more about interest groups by understanding the role that identity plays when these groups act. Through this research, the salience of gender identity is made clear. Unfortunately, large-scale surveys of interest groups often miss the significance of this variable. For example, like most other institutionalized political actors, CWA and IWF seek media attention to promote their beliefs and goals. But to really understand the nature of their media influence, it is important not just to consider that these organizations "talk with people from the press and media,"[24] but to know *who* is talking to the press for them and why. In both cases, these groups choose women to make public statements to give them credibility and to try to change the way the public thinks about women's interests. This insight offers a more textured and richer explanation of the communications strategies of the two groups. In addition, it suggests that their interactions with media outlets may be shaped by their desire to have women be prominent spokespeople.

Far from dismissing conservative women leaders as political pawns and victims of false consciousness, feminists need to take seriously how women are represented by groups like CWA and IWF. Since the media give them face and air time, and since these organizations have close ties to powerful members of Congress, other conservative leaders, and Bush's Republican administration, we should expect that they will indeed be taken seriously as policy advocates for women. Perhaps for this reason alone, scholars should continue to pursue answers to questions about this growing force of conservative women.

APPENDIX A
Data and Methods

I CONDUCTED TWENTY semistructured, open-ended, in-depth interviews with leaders and professional staff of CWA and IWF between 1998 and 2002 (see appendix B) and coded all interviews using NUDIST and INVIVO qualitative data analysis programs. Since my research concerns organizational founding goals and representational strategies, I pursued and completed interviews with those most likely to be responsible for such duties: the organizations' presidents, executive directors, lobbyists, public relations directors, and editors. These semistructured interviews lasted from one and a half to four hours each. All were taped, and all but two were on the record.

An extensive qualitative data analysis of the organizations' periodicals and Web site pages, 1981–2004 (see appendix B), was also conducted. Publications were first analyzed for recurring themes and issues. Next, I systematically coded all articles related to the organizations' general missions, views on feminism, and other policy issues presented in this book. CWA puts out its glossy *Family Voice* on a monthly basis, and, until 2003 IWF published a quarterly journal entitled the *Women's Quarterly* and a quarterly newsletter called *Ex Femina*. These were circulated to all members and contributors, but now its literature is posted in electronic format on its Web site. In addition, relevant documents such as press releases, amicus briefs, pamphlets, and special reports were examined and are appropriately cited. While IWF declares in its periodicals that not all of its contributors reflect its views, the articles were ideologically consistent and mostly written by people closely affiliated with the organization, such as IWF advisory board members. As such, I attribute the content of these publications to the organizations themselves.

Finally, to get a clearer sense of how these organizations relate to their members and the public, I attended two national CWA conventions—September 19–21, 1996, at the Sheraton Washington Hotel in Washington, DC, and September 24–27, 1998, at the Radisson Plaza Hotel in Alexandria, Virginia—and participated in a day-long IWF conference entitled "Scared Sick?" at the National Press Club in Washington, DC, on February 17, 1999. I was also an invited participant at "Core Connections: Women, Religion and Public Policy," a symposium held October 8–9, 1999, at the John F. Kennedy School of Government at Harvard University; associates from both organizations were present and participated in this conference. In all of these public gatherings, I socialized with members and associates, ate meals with them, and in many circumstances, told them I was doing a study of their organizations. As with the interview process, all of my interactions were amicable; most of the women seemed quite pleased that I was conducting this study and, surprisingly, none asked me to detail my research questions or what I expected to find. While the specific data analyzed for this project come from interviews and organizational literature, this method of participant observation afforded me a greater ability to understand and interact with antifeminist women leaders and broadened my general understanding about how the organizations work.

APPENDIX B
Interviews and Documents

Primary Documents*

CWA Publications
CWA Newsletter (24 issues, 1981–1991)
Family Voice (53 issues, 1991–2000)

CWA Web Page
Core Issues page (pornography and sanctity of life links, 2000–2004)

IWF Publications
Agenda for Women (4 issues, 2002–2005)
Ex Femina (24 issues, 1996–2002)
Women's Quarterly (32 issues, 1994–2001)

IWF Web Page
Issues page (women and work, sexual harassment, violence against women, health/science links, 1999–2004)

---

* This list does not include occasional pamphlets, amicus briefs, and press releases, which are specifically cited in the text.

Interviews

Concerned Women for America

Conducted in Person

Rosaline Bush, director of publications and research, October 8, 1998
Patty Dahnke, national field director, October 7, 1998
Barbara Franceski, director of broadcast and media, October 29, 1998
Laurel MacLeod, legislative director, August 18, 1998
Carmen Pate, president, August 18, 1998
Seriah Rein, NJ state area representative, August 6, 1998
Jan Roberto, board member, September 25, 1998
Michael Schwartz, vice president for government relations,
    December 7, 2001

Conducted by Phone

Kathy Arrington, board member, October 14, 1998
Kenda Bartlett, special assistant to the chairman, November 4, 1998
Angela Lipsit, prayer action chapter leader in WV, October 27, 1998

Independent Women's Forum

Conducted in Person

Anonymous, board member, February 19, 1999
Anonymous, IWF staff, January 20, 2002
Anita Blair, vice president and counsel, October 30, 1998
Barbara Ledeen, executive director for policy, October 30, 1998
Sally Satel, science advisor, February 17, 1999
Ricky Silberman, board president, November 11, 1998
Christine Stolba, senior fellow, December 5, 2001

Conducted by Phone

Wendy Gramm, board member, January 20, 1999
Kimberly Schuld, special projects manager, November 24, 1998

NOTES

Introduction

1. See the front of this book for the ad.
2. This title is a play on the "Take Back the Night" activities run by feminist activists to draw attention to violence against women.
3. For example, the ad argues that among the "ten most common feminist myths" is that "one in four women in college has been the victim of rape or attempted rape." IWF contends that this "mother of all factoids" was perpetrated by *Ms.* magazine and researcher Mary Koss in a story about Koss's survey research. Scoffing that *Ms.* publisher and "hard-line" feminist Gloria Steinem "hand-picked" Koss to complete the research, IWF claims that reporting on the study failed to acknowledge that most girls did not realize they had been raped when asked about their experiences and thus the data are overblown. IWF's ad proceeds to acknowledge that "rape is a uniquely horrible crime...[but]...women will not be helped by hyperbole and hysteria."
4. Stanley Kurtz, *Feminist against Speech* (May 24, 2001), www.nationalreview.com/comment; John Leo, "Miffing the Myth Makers," *U.S. News and World Report* (June 4, 2001): 14; Dana Mulhauser, "National Group Rallies Students Who Question Campus Feminism," *Chronicle of Higher Education* 5 (October 2001): A37; Katha Pollitt, "Mad Bad Ads," *Nation* (June 7, 2001): 4.
5. For exceptions, see Barbara Spindel, "Conservatism as the 'Sensible Middle': The Independent Women's Forum, Politics and the Media," *Social Text* 21, no. 4 (Winter 2003): 99–125; Jean Hardisty, *Mobilizing Resentment: Conservative Resurgence from the John Birch Society to the Promise Keepers* (Boston: Beacon, 1999); Susan E. Marshall, "Confrontation and Co-Optation in Antifeminist Organizations," in *Feminist Organizations*, ed. Myra Marx Ferree and Patricia Yancey Martin (Philadelphia, PA: Temple University Press, 1995), 323–38. See

also Rebecca Klatch, *Women of the New Right* (Philadelphia, PA: Temple University Press, 1987), for a pioneering study of conservative women.

6. Richard Morin and Claudia Deane, "Women's Forum Challenges Feminists, Gains Influence," *Washington Post* (May 1, 2001): A6.

7. Leonie Huddy, "Feminists and Feminism in the News," in *Women, Media and Politics*, ed. Pippa Norris (New York: Oxford University Press, 1997), 183–204.

8. Karen Beckwith, "Lancashire Women against Pit Closures: Women's Standing in a Men's Movement," *Signs* 21, no. 4 (Summer 1996): 1034–63.

9. For studies of conservative politics, see Clyde Wilcox, "Of Movements and Metaphors: The Co-Evolution of the Christian Right and the GOP," paper presented at the Christian Conservative Movement and American Democracy meeting, Russell Sage Foundation, NY, April 2007; Lisa McGirr, *Suburban Warriors: The Origins of the New American Right* (Princeton, NJ: Princeton University Press, 2001); Lee Edwards, *The Conservative Revolution* (New York: Free Press, 1999); William Martin, *With God on Our Side: The Rise of the Religious Right in America* (New York: Broadway, 1996); Sara Diamond, *Roads to Dominion: Right-Wing Movements and Political Power in the United States* (New York: Guilford, 1995); John C. Green et al. (eds.), *Religion and the Culture Wars: Dispatches from the Front* (Lanham, MD: Rowman and Littlefield, 1996); Mark J. Rozell and Clyde Wilcox (eds.), *God at the Grass Roots: The Christian Right in the 1994 Elections* (Lanham, MD: Rowman and Littlefield, 1995); Matthew Moen, *The Transformation of the Christian Right* (Tuscaloosa: University of Alabama Press, 1992); Allen D. Hertzke, *Representing God in Washington* (Knoxville: University of Tennessee Press, 1988); Pamela Johnston Conover and Virginia Gray, *Feminism and the New Right: Conflict over the American Family* (New York: Praeger, 1983); Alan Crawford, *Thunder on the Right: The "New Right" and the Politics of Resentment* (New York: Pantheon, 1980); Seymour Martin Lipset and Earl Raab, *The Politics of Unreason: Right-Wing Extremism in America, 1790–1970* (New York: Harper and Row, 1970).

10. For example, in 1980, there were 908 women state legislators (12.1%); in 2008, there were 1,741 (23.6%). In the U.S. Congress, the number has risen from 17 women in the House and Senate in 1980 (3.2%) to 86, or 16.1%, of all members in 2006. The figures can be found at www.cawp.rutgers.edu, the Web site for the Center for American Women and Politics, Rutgers University, New Brunswick, NJ.

11. M. Margaret Conway, David W. Ahern, and Gertrude A. Steuernagel, *Women and Public Policy* (Washington, DC: Congressional Quarterly Press, 2004); Dorothy McBride Stetson, *Women's Rights in the U.S.A.: Policy Debates and Gender Roles* (New York: Routledge, 2004); Debra Dodson et al., *Voices, Views, Votes: The Impact of Women in the 103rd Congress* (New Brunswick, NJ: Center for the American Woman and Politics, 1995); Myra Marx Ferree and Patricia Yancey Martin (eds.), *Feminist Organizations: Harvest of the New Women's Movement* (Philadelphia, PA: Temple University Press, 1995); Marlene Gerber Fried, *Abortion to Reproductive Freedom: Transforming a Movement* (Boston:

South End, 1990); Joyce Gelb and Marian Lief Palley, *Women and Public Policies* (Princeton, NJ: Princeton University Press, 1987); Ellen Boneparth and Emily Stoper (eds.), *Women, Power and Policy: Toward the Year 2000* (New York: Pergamon, 1988).

12. A 2006 CBS News poll found that 65% of women reported that the women's movement has made their lives better, but in that same study, only 27% of women considered themselves to be feminists.

13. Lee Ann Banaszak (ed.), *The U.S. Women's Movement in Global Perspective* (Lanham, MD: Rowman and Littlefield, 2006); Rachel Roth, *Making Women Pay: The Hidden Costs of Fetal Rights* (Ithaca, NY: Cornell University Press, 2003); Ruth Rosen, *The World Split Open: How the Modern Women's Movement Changed America* (New York: Viking, 2000); Susan Brownmiller, *In Our Time: A Memoir of a Revolution* (New York: Dial, 1999); Cathy Cohen, Kathleen Jones, and Joan Tronto, *Women Transforming Politics: An Alternative Reader* (New York: New York University Press, 1997); Ferree and Martin, *Feminist Organizations: Harvest of the New Women's Movement*; Patricia Yancey Martin, "Rethinking Feminist Organizations," *Gender and Society* 4, no. 2 (June 1990): 182–206; Alice Echols, *Daring to Be Bad: Radical Feminism in America 1967–1975* (Minneapolis: University of Minnesota Press, 1989); Ann Bookman and Sandra Morgen, *Women and the Politics of Empowerment* (Philadelphia, PA: Temple University Press, 1988); Mary Fainsod Katzenstein and Carol McClurg Mueller (eds.), *The Women's Movement of the United States and Western Europe: Consciousness, Political Opportunity and Public Policy* (Philadelphia, PA: Temple University Press, 1987).

14. Martin, "Rethinking Feminist Organizations."

15. Debra Dodson, *The Impact of Women in Congress* (Oxford: Oxford University Press, 2006); Susan Carroll, "Representing Women: Congresswomen's Perceptions of Their Representational Roles," in *Women Transforming Congress*, ed. Cindy Simon Rosenthal (Norman: University of Oklahoma Press, 2002–3), 50–68; Jane Mansbridge, "Should Blacks Represent Blacks and Women Represent Women? A Contingent 'Yes,'" *Journal of Politics* 61, no. 3 (August 1999): 628–57; Anne Phillips, *The Politics of Presence* (Oxford: Oxford University Press, 1995); Will Kymlicka, *Multicultural Citizenship: A Liberal Theory of Minority Rights* (New York: Oxford University Press, 1995); Hanna Fenichel Pitkin, *The Concept of Representation* (Berkeley: University of California Press, 1967).

16. Beckwith, "Lancashire Women against Pit Closures."

17. Dara Strolovitch, *Affirmative Advocacy: Race, Class and Gender in Interest Group Politics* (Chicago, IL: University of Chicago Press, 2007); Allan J. Cigler and Burdett A. Loomis (eds.), *Interest Group Politics* (Washington, DC: Congressional Quarterly Press, 1998); Kay Lehman Schlozman and John T. Tierney, *Organized Interests and American Democracy* (New York: Harper and Row, 1986); Theodore J. Lowi, *The End of Liberalism* (New York: Norton, 1979); E. E. Schattschneider, *The Semi-Sovereign People* (New York: Holt, Rinehart

and Winston, 1960); David B. Truman, *The Governmental Process: Political Interests and Public Opinion* (New York: Knopf, 1951).

18. Gayatri Spivak, *Outside in the Teaching Machine* (New York: Routledge, 1993).

19. Deborah Stone, *Policy Paradox: The Art of Political Decision Making* (New York: Norton, 2002); Sidney Tarrow, "Mentalities, Political Cultures, and Collective Action Frames," in *Frontiers in Social Movement Theory*, ed. Aldon D. Morris and Carol McClurg Mueller (New Haven, CT: Yale University Press, 1992), 174–202; David A. Snow and Robert D. Benford, "Ideology, Frame Resonance, and Participant Mobilization," *International Social Movement Research* 1 (1988): 197–217.

20. Myra Marx Ferree and Carol McClurg Mueller, "Feminism and the Women's Movement: A Global Perspective," in *The Blackwell Companion to Social Movements*, ed. David A. Snow, Sarah A. Soule, and Hanspeter Kriesi (Malden, MA: Blackwell, 2004), 576–607; Stone, *Policy Paradox*.

21. David A. Snow et al., "Frame Alignment Processes, Micromobilization, and Movement Participation," *American Sociological Review* 51 (August 1986): 464–81.

22. Maryann Barakso and Brian Schaffner, "Winning Coverage: News Media Portrayals of the Women's Movement, 1969–2004," *Harvard International Journal of Press/Politics* 11, no. 4 (2006): 22–44; Huddy, "Feminists and Feminism in the News," 183–204.

23. Center for the Advancement of Women, *Progress and Perils: New Agenda for Women* (June 2003) (www.advancewomen.org).

24. Leonie Huddy, Francis K. Neely, and Marilyn R. LaFay, "The Polls: Trends: Support for the Women's Movement," *Public Opinion Quarterly* 64 (2000): 309–50.

25. In the aforementioned 2006 CBS News poll, 15% of women said that calling someone a feminist was a compliment, 14% claimed it was an insult, and 65% reported that it was a neutral action.

26. Ronnee Schreiber, "Playing 'Femball': Conservative Women's Organizations and Political Representation in the United States," in *Right-Wing Women: From Conservatives to Extremists around the World*, ed. Paola Bacchetta and Margaret Power (New York: Routledge, 2002), 211–24.

27. Schreiber, "Playing 'Femball.'"

28. Susan E. Marshall, "Marilyn vs. Hillary: Women's Place in New Right Politics," *Women and Politics* 16, no. 1 (1996): 55–75.

29. It is important to briefly note my role as a researcher in this project. As a feminist scholar and activist, I faced some challenges in approaching research subjects and establishing my legitimacy as an "objective" analyst. My initial concern—gaining access to conservative women—was quickly allayed. To my surprise, all but one person I asked granted me an interview (eighteen of which were on the record). I attribute this positive response to presenting myself as a researcher seeking to expand the field of women and politics scholarship by representing conservative women's points of view.

Conducting interviews and attending conferences with people whose ideas are so divergent from your own also provide a true test of one's ability to gather information and insights in a clear and systematic fashion. It is my belief that I was able to accomplish this goal in part because the activists were helpful, relatively easy to engage, and generally uninterested in where I stood on the issues. That is, very few asked me about my political values and when they did, none seemed particularly concerned about them. Conducting the interviews on tape and on the record also made the women feel more secure: there was evidence of our conversations. Given the relative dearth of research on this topic, interviewees were also pleased that someone cared to speak with them. For an insightful discussion of studying a politically resistant community, see Rebecca Klatch, "The Methodological Problems of Studying a Politically Resistant Community," *Studies in Qualitative Sociology* 1 (1988): 73–88.

30. Robert K. Yin, *Case Study Research: Design and Methods* (Beverly Hills, CA: Sage, 1984).

31. Many consider Eagle Forum, founded and still run by Phyllis Schlafly, to be a conservative women's organization. Although it is led by a woman and is well known for its successful opposition to the ERA, it does not specifically consider itself to be a women's organization and thus was not chosen for this study.

32. Maryann Barakso, *Governing NOW: Grassroots Activism in the National Organization for Women* (Ithaca, NY: Cornell University Press, 2004); Ferree and Martin, *Feminist Organizations: Harvest of the New Women's Movement*; Cohen, Jones, and Tronto, *Women Transforming Politics: An Alternative Reader*; Shane Phelan, "(Be)Coming Out: Lesbian Identity and Politics," *Signs: Journal of Women in Culture and Society* 18, no. 4 (Summer 1993): 765–90; Chandra Talpade Mohanty, "Under Western Eyes: Feminist Scholarship and Colonial Discourses," in *Third World Women and the Politics of Feminism*, ed. Chandra Talpade Mohanty, Ann Russo, and Lourdes Torres (Bloomington: Indiana University Press, 1991), 51–80; bell hooks, *Yearning: Race, Gender and Cultural Politics* (Boston: South End, 1990); Patricia Hill Collins, *Black Feminist Thought: Knowledge, Consciousness and the Politics of Empowerment* (New York: Routledge, 1990); Anne N. Costain, "Representing Women: The Transition from Social Movement to Interest Group," in *Women, Power and Policy: Toward the Year 2000*, ed. Ellen Boneparth and Emily Stoper (New York: Pergamon, 1988), 26–47; Katzenstein and Mueller, *The Women's Movement of the United States and Western Europe*; Anne N. Costain and W. Douglas Costain, "Strategy and Tactics of the Women's Movement in the United States: The Role of Political Parties," in *The Women's Movement of the United States and Western Europe*, ed. Mary Fainsod Katzenstein and Carol McClurg Mueller (Philadelphia, PA: Temple University Press, 1987), 196–214; Gelb and Palley, *Women and Public Policies*; Jo Freeman, *The Politics of Women's Liberation* (New York: McKay, 1976).

33. Laurie A. Rhodebeck, "The Structure of Men's and Women's Feminist Orienta-tions," *Gender and Society* 10, no. 4 (August 1996): 386–403; Anne Hildreth and Ellen M. Dran, "Explaining Women's Differences in Abortion Opinion: The Role of Gender Consciousness," *Women and Politics* 14, no. 1 (1994): 31–33; Sue Tolleson-Rinehart, *Gender Consciousness and Politics* (New York: Routledge, 1992); Pamela Conover, "Feminists and the Gender Gap," *Journal of Politics* 50, no. 4 (November 1988): 985–1009; Arthur H. Miller, Anne Hildreth, and Grace L. Simmons, "The Mobilization of Gender Group Consciousness," in *The Political Interests of Gender*, ed. Kathleen B. Jones and Anna G. Jonasdottir (London: Sage, 1988), 106–34; Patricia Gurin, "Women's Gender Conscious-ness," *Public Opinion Quarterly* 49 (1985): 143–63; Ethel Klein, *Gender Poli-tics: From Consciousness to Mass Politics* (Cambridge, MA: Harvard University Press, 1984).

34. Diamond, *Roads to Dominion*.

35. James L. Guth et al., "Onward Christian Soldiers: Religious Activist Groups in American Politics," in *Interest Group Politics*, ed. Allan J. Cigler and Burdett A. Loomis (Washington, DC: Congressional Quarterly Press, 1994), 55–76.

36. Cynthia Burack and Jyl J. Josephson, "Women and the American New Right: Feminist Interventions," *Women and Politics* 24, no. 2 (2002): 69–90; Sylvia Bashevkin, *Women on the Defensive: Living through Conservative Times* (Chicago, IL: University of Chicago Press, 1998); Conover and Gray, *Feminism and the New Right: Conflict over the American Family*.

37. Andrea Dworkin, *Right-Wing Women* (New York: Perigee, 1983).

38. Wendy Kaminer, "Will Class Trump Gender?" *American Prospect* (November–December 1996): 44–52.

39. Dworkin, *Right-Wing Women*, 35.

40. Steven Gardiner, "Concerned Women for America—A Case Study," *Fight the Right Action Kit* (1998), www.sexuality.org/1/activism.

41. Conover, "Feminists and the Gender Gap," 1005.

42. Marshall, "Marilyn vs. Hillary: Women's Place in New Right Politics"; Kathleen Blee, *Women of the Klan: Racism and Gender in the 1920's* (Berkeley: University of California Press, 1991); Kristin Luker, *Abortion and the Politics of Motherhood* (Berkeley: University of California Press, 1984); Jane Mansbridge, *Why We Lost the ERA* (Chicago, IL: University of Chicago Press, 1986); David W. Brady and Kent L. Tedin, "Ladies in Pink: Religion and Political Ideol-ogy in the Anti-ERA Movement," *Social Science Quarterly* 56 (March 1976): 564–75.

43. Linda Kintz, *Between Jesus and the Marketplace: The Emotions That Matter in Right-Wing America* (Durham, NC: Duke University Press, 1997); Marshall, "Marilyn vs. Hillary: Women's Place in New Right Politics."

44. Barbara Norrander, "The Evolution of the Gender Gap," *Public Opinion Quar-terly* 63, no. 4 (Winter 1999): 566–77; Carol M. Mueller, *The Politics of the Gender Gap: The Social Construction of Political Influence* (Beverly Hills, CA: Sage, 1988).

45. Dworkin, *Right-Wing Women*, 35.

Chapter Two

1. Rebecca Klatch, *A Generation Divided: The New Left, the New Right and the 1960's* (Berkeley: University of California Press, 1999).
2. Thomas Jablonsky, "Female Opposition: The Anti-Suffrage Campaign," in *Votes for Women*, ed. Jean H. Baker (New York: Oxford University Press, 2002), 118–29.
3. Susan E. Marshall, "Ladies against Women: Mobilization Dilemmas of Anti-feminist Women," *Social Problems* 32, no. 4 (April 1985): 348–62.
4. Susan Marshall, *Splintered Sisterhood: Gender and Class in the Campaign against Woman Suffrage* (Madison: University of Wisconsin Press, 1997).
5. Mrs. Arthur Dodge, "Woman Suffrage Opposed to Woman's Rights," *American Academy of Political and Social Science* 56 (1914): 104.
6. Jablonsky, "Female Opposition," 127.
7. Marshall, "Ladies against Women."
8. Marshall, *Splintered Sisterhood*; Louise Stevenson, "Women Anti-Suffragists in the 1915 Massachusetts Campaign," *New England Quarterly* 52, no. 1 (March 1979): 80–93.
9. Marshall, "Ladies against Women," 350.
10. Marshall, "Ladies against Women," 355.
11. Marshall, *Splintered Sisterhood*.
12. Blee, *Women of the Klan: Racism and Gender in the 1920's*.
13. Blee, *Women of the Klan: Racism and Gender in the 1920's*.
14. Blee, *Women of the Klan: Racism and Gender in the 1920's*.
15. Blee, *Women of the Klan: Racism and Gender in the 1920's*, 69.
16. June Melby Benowitz, *Days of Discontent: American Women and Right-Wing Politics* (DeKalb: Northern Illinois University Press, 2002); Glen Jeansonne, *Women of the Far Right: The Mothers' Movement and World War II* (Chicago, IL: University of Chicago Press, 1996).
17. Jeansonne, *Women of the Far Right*, 7.
18. Jeansonne, *Women of the Far Right*.
19. Kathleen Blee, "Mothers in Race-Hate Movements," in *The Politics of Motherhood*, ed. Alexis Jetter, Annelise Orleck, and Diana Taylor (Hanover, NH: University Press of New England, 1997), 247–56.
20. Kathleen Blee, *Inside Organized Racism: Women and Men in the Hate Movement* (Berkeley: University of California Press, 2002).
21. McGirr, *Suburban Warriors: The Origins of the New American Right*; Rick Perlstein, *Before the Storm* (New York: Hill and Wang, 2001); Klatch, *A Generation Divided*.
22. McGirr, *Suburban Warriors: The Origins of the New American Right*, 87.
23. Klatch, *Women of the New Right*.
24. Klatch, *A Generation Divided*, 265.
25. Phyllis Schlafly, *A Choice, Not an Echo* (Alton, IL: Pere Marquette, 1964).
26. Klatch, *A Generation Divided*, 266.

27. Carol Felsenthal, *Phyllis Schlafly: The Sweetheart of the Silent Majority* (Chicago, IL: Regnery Gateway, 1981).

28. Mansbridge, *Why We Lost the ERA*.

29. See the organization's Web site: www.cblpolicyinstitute.org.

30. See the organization's Web site: www.enlightenedwomen.org.

31. See the organization's Web site: www.sba-list.org.

32. Spindel, "Conservatism as the 'Sensible Middle.'"

33. Ann Coulter, *Godless: The Church of Liberalism* (New York: Crown Forum, 2006), 102–3.

34. Ann Coulter, *How to Talk to a Liberal (If You Must)* (New York: Crown Forum, 2004), 324.

35. Coulter, *How to Talk to a Liberal (If You Must)*, 325.

36. Christina Hoff Sommers, *Who Stole Feminism? How Women Have Betrayed Women* (New York: Touchstone, 1994).

37. Sommers, *Who Stole Feminism?*, 178.

38. Bernard Chapin, "Post Super Bowl Feminism: An Interview with Christina Hoff Sommers," *American Spectator Online* (February 2, 2007), www.aei.org.

39. This quote was accessed on May 20, 1997, at www.iwf.org.

40. Spindel, "Conservatism as the 'Sensible Middle'"; Susan Faludi, *Backlash: The Undeclared War against Women* (New York: Crown, 1991); Dworkin, *Right-Wing Women*.

41. See www.mediatransparency.org.

42. Wilcox, "Of Movements and Metaphors."

43. Tim LaHaye and Beverly LaHaye, *The Act of Marriage: The Beauty of Sexual Love* (Grand Rapids, MI: Zondervan, 1998).

44. This information was found on the Web site of People for the American Way: www.pfaw.org.

45. See "Statement of Concerned Women for America on the Passing of Dr. Jerry Falwell" at www.cwfa.org.

46. See "The Next Conservatism: A Series by Paul M. Weyrich" at www.cwfa.org.

47. IWF, "Hot Topics," *Media*, Press Release, June 14, 2004, www.iwf.org/media/media.

48. MacLeod interview.

49. Wilcox, "Of Movements and Metaphors."

50. Concerned Women for America, *Welcome to Concerned Women for America*, Membership Packet (Washington, DC: Concerned Women for America, 1995).

51. Green et al., *Religion and the Culture Wars*.

52. Robert Wuthnow, "Political Rebirth of American Evangelicals," in *The New Christian Right*, ed. Robert C. Liebman and Robert Wuthnow (New York: Aldine, 1983), 168–85.

53. Wuthnow, "Political Rebirth," 183.

54. Hardisty, *Mobilizing Resentment*.

55. John C. Green, "The Christian Right and the 1994 Elections: An Overview," in *God at the Grass Roots*, ed. Mark J. Rozell and Clyde Wilcox (Lanham, MD: Rowman and Littlefield, 1995), 1–18.

56. Moen, *The Transformation of the Christian Right*.

57. Martin, *With God on Our Side: The Rise of the Religious Right in America*.

58. Wilcox, "Of Movements and Metaphors"; Edwards, *The Conservative Revolution*; Diamond, *Roads to Dominion*; Green, "The Christian Right and the 1994 Elections."

59. Hardisty, *Mobilizing Resentment*; Diamond, *Roads to Dominion*; Klatch, *Women of the New Right*.

60. Some contest the membership count given by CWA. On its Web site, www.now.org, NOW—a feminist women's group—also claims to have 500,000 members. CWA contends that NOW really has fewer than 100,000.

61. Michael Schwartz, "Marriage Wins the Day in Congress," www.cwfa.org (July 23, 2004).

62. Neither CWA nor IWF has official data on the race of its members. However, when I asked them about their constituents' demographics, interviewees noted that most of their members or associates were white women.

63. Janice Shaw Crouse, "Abortion: America's Staggering Hidden Loss," *Beverly LaHaye Institute Data Digest*, www.cwfa.org.

64. See www.fec.gov.

65. Andrew Greeley and Michael Hout, *The Truth about Conservative Christians: Who They Are and What They Think* (Chicago, IL: University of Chicago Press, 2006), note that white conservative Protestants (a label they use to refer to what others call evangelicals and fundamentalists), such as those who comprise CWA, account for about 26% of the adult American population. Christian Right scholar John Green argues that evangelicals' high degree of religious commitment allows for effective mobilization on the basis of moral and religious appeals ("The Christian Right and the 1994 Elections"). In addition, others have shown that conservative religious women are especially motivated to political action through their religious beliefs. For example, a survey conducted by Princeton Survey Research Associates for the Center for Gender Equality found that 40% of "born again women" say religion has influenced their political activism as compared to only 28% of women who attend religious services but do not identify with this traditionally conservative label (Center for the Advancement of Women, 1999, *The Impact of Religious Organizations on Gender Equality: A Report of Findings from a National Survey of Women* (www.advancewomen.org).

66. See www.cwfa.org.

67. Moen, *The Transformation of the Christian Right*; Hertzke, *Representing God in Washington*.

68. Silberman interview.

69. The acronym WIN is now used by a group of prochoice Democratic women. See www.winonline.org.

70. Silberman died in 2007 from cancer.

71. Independent Women's Forum, *Who Are We? The Future*, Recruitment Pamphlet (Washington, DC: Independent Women's Forum, 1996).

72. Silberman interview.

73. Spindel, "Conservatism as the 'Sensible Middle,'" 121.

74. Spindel, "Conservatism as the 'Sensible Middle.'"

75. Anonymous interview with IWF leader.

76. "IWF Agenda for Women, 2005," 15.

77. www.iwf.org/campuscorner.

78. This phrase comes from a direct-mail letter that IWF sent out. The letter is dated May 21, 2007.

79. Hardisty, *Mobilizing Resentment*, 91.

80. Elizabeth Fox-Genovese, *Feminism Is Not the Story of My Life: How Today's Feminist Elite Has Lost Touch with the Real Concerns of Women* (New York: Talese/Doubleday, 1995); Sommers, *Who Stole Feminism?*; Daphne Patai and Noretta Koertge, *Professing Feminism: Cautionary Tales from the Strange World of Women's Studies* (New York: Basic, 1994); Katie Roiphe, *The Morning After: Sex, Fear and Feminism on Campus* (Boston: Little, Brown, 1993).

Chapter Three

1. Faye Ginsburg, *Contested Lives: The Abortion Debate in an American Community* (Berkeley: University of California Press, 1989); Luker, *Abortion and the Politics of Motherhood*.

2. Judith Butler, "Contingent Foundations: Feminism and the Question of 'Postmodernism,'" in *Feminists Theorize the Political*, ed. Judith Butler and Joan Scott (New York: Routledge, 1992), 15.

3. Roth, *Making Women Pay: The Hidden Costs of Fetal Rights*; Cohen, Jones, and Tronto, *Women Transforming Politics: An Alternative Reader*; Phelan, "(Be)Coming Out"; Mohanty, "Under Western Eyes: Feminist Scholarship and Colonial Discourses"; Collins, *Black Feminist Thought: Knowledge, Consciousness and the Politics of Empowerment*; Rochelle Lefkowitz and Ann Withorn, *For Crying Out Loud* (New York: Pilgrim, 1986).

4. Diana Fuss, *Essentially Speaking* (New York: Routledge, 1989), 2.

5. Iris Marion Young, "Gender as Seriality: Thinking about Women as a Social Collective," *Signs* 19, no. 3 (Spring 1994): 713–38; Phelan, "(Be)Coming Out"; Spivak, *Outside in the Teaching Machine*; Fuss, *Essentially Speaking*.

6. Spivak, *Outside in the Teaching Machine*, ix.

7. Spivak, *Outside in the Teaching Machine*, 4.

8. Blair interview.

9. Blair interview.

10. Satel interview.

11. Rein interview.

12. Bartlett interview. The women to whom Bartlett is referring are the president of NOW, a founder of Feminist Majority Foundation, and the executive director of NARAL, respectively.

13. Anonymous IWF staff interview.

14. This quote comes from the home page of IWF's Web site, www.iwf.org.

15. While CWA uses the term "Christians," it is specifically referring to conservative evangelical Protestant and fundamentalist Christians, the religious group that comprises most of its membership. See Guth et al., "Onward Christian Soldiers."

16. Franceski interview.

17. Beverly LaHaye, *The Desires of a Woman's Heart* (Wheaton, IL: Tyndale, 1993), 138; emphasis added.

18. LaHaye, *The Desires of a Woman's Heart*, 183.

19. Ann Coulter, *Slander: Liberal Lies about the American Right* (New York: Three Rivers, 2003); Bernard Goldberg, *Arrogance: Rescuing America from the Media Elite* (New York: Warner, 2003).

20. Stolba interview.

21. Laura Flanders, "Conservative Women Are Right for Media Mainstream," *Extra!* (March–April 1996): 1–3.

22. Ronnee Schreiber, "'Will the Real Media Darlings Please Rise?' An Analysis of Print Coverage of Feminist and Conservative Women's Organizations," paper presented at the Western Political Science Association Meetings, March 2006.

23. Blair interview.

24. Gramm interview.

25. Spindel, "Conservatism as the 'Sensible Middle.'"

26. Roberto interview.

27. Bush interview.

28. See www.cwfa.org/leadership.asp.

29. Megan Rosenfeld, "Feminist Fatales: This Conservative Women's Group Has Traditionalists Seething," *Washington Post* (November 30, 1995): D1.

30. Arrington interview.

31. MacLeod interview.

32. Bartlett interview.

33. Alexis Jetter, Annelise Orleck, and Diana Taylor (eds.), *The Politics of Motherhood: Activist Voices from Left to Right* (Hanover, NH: University Press of New England, 1997).

34. Franceski interview.

35. Pate interview.

36. LaHaye, *The Desires of a Woman's Heart*, 80.

37. Blair interview.

38. Anonymous IWF staff interview; emphasis added.

39. Dodson, *The Impact of Women in Congress*; Michelle Swers, *The Difference Women Make* (Chicago, IL: University of Chicago Press, 2002); Sue Thomas, *How Women Legislate* (New York: Oxford University Press, 1994); Debra Dodson and Susan Carroll, *Reshaping the Agenda: Women in State Legislatures* (New Brunswick, NJ: Center for the American Woman and Politics, 1991).

40. Kate O'Beirne, "The GOP's Answer to Hillary," *Women's Quarterly* (Summer 1998): 11.

41. In addition to IWF, these organizations include the Center for Equal Opportunity, the American Enterprise Institute, and the Campaign for a Color-Blind America.

42. Rein interview.

43. Dodson, *The Impact of Women in Congress*; Swers, *The Difference Women Make*; Thomas, *How Women Legislate*; Dodson and Carroll, *Reshaping the Agenda*.

44. MacLeod interview.

45. Kathleen Dolan, "Women Candidates: What We Know, What We Need to Know," paper presented at the Annual Meeting of the Midwest Political Science Association, Chicago, IL, April 2006.

46. I use the term "traditional areas of concern" here to mirror the language used by Dodson and Carroll, *Reshaping the Agenda*. They use the term *traditional* to reflect national public opinion among women in the United States over the past few decades, and thus the meaning of "traditional" here is limited in its historical and cultural manifestations.

47. Dodson, *The Impact of Women in Congress*; Swers, *The Difference Women Make*; Dodson and Carroll, *Reshaping the Agenda*.

48. Carroll, "Representing Women: Congresswomen's Perceptions of Their Representational Roles."

49. See www.sba-list.org/index.htm for more information about the PAC.

50. Beckwith, "Lancashire Women against Pit Closures."

51. Fuss, *Essentially Speaking*.

52. Young, "Gender as Seriality."

Chapter Four

1. These data can be found on NCADV's Web site: www.ncadv.org/aboutus.php.

2. VAWA allocates federal funds to state and local sexual assault and domestic violence programs, training, and services. It also established the Office on Violence against Women in the U.S. Department of Justice. Prior to this law, federal efforts were more narrowly focused and failed to convey a sense that dealing with violence against women should be a national, bipartisan endeavor.

3. Deborah Rhode, *Justice and Gender* (Cambridge, MA: Harvard University Press, 1989), 244.

4. Cathy Young, *Domestic Violence: An In-Depth Analysis*, IWF Position Paper (September 2005), www.iwf.org/files/50c58ddao9fl6c86b2c652aao47944f6.pdf.

5. Lisa Duggan and Nan Hunter, *Sex Wars* (New York: Routledge, 1995).

6. Candida Royalle, "Porn in the USA," in *Feminism and Pornography*, ed. Drucilla Cornell (Oxford: Oxford University Press, 2000), 540–50; Wendy McElroy, *XXX: A Woman's Right to Pornography* (New York: St. Martin's, 1995).

7. Ann L. Pastore and Kathleen Maguire, eds., *Sourcebook of Criminal Justice Statistics* (2003), www.albany.edu/sourcebook. That study also found that 52% of

women supported laws forbidding the distribution of pornography to persons under the age of eighteen; only 4% favored no laws at all.

8. Catharine MacKinnon and Andrea Dworkin, *In Harm's Way* (Cambridge, MA: Harvard University Press, 1998).

9. Catharine MacKinnon, "Only Words," in *Feminism and Pornography*, ed. Drucilla Cornell (Oxford: Oxford University Press, 2000), 97.

10. For example, CWA's Janice Crouse criticizes MacKinnon's views on heterosexual sex in "Human Sexuality through Different Lenses," which can be found at www.cwfa.org.

11. Rosaline Bush, "Caught in the Web of Porn: From Victims to Victors," *Family Voice* (May 1997): 8.

12. Arrington interview.

13. Wendy Wright, "Victims of Pornography," *Core Issues: Pornography*, January 1, 2002, Concerned Women for America, www.cwfa.org.

14. Nina George Hacker, "Porn on the Internet: Is It Free Speech?" *Family Voice* (March 1997): 6.

15. Hacker, "Porn on the Internet," 10.

16. Concerned Women for America, "Hefner: A Kinsey Disciple," *Family Voice* (June 1997): 14.

17. Bush, "Caught in the Web of Porn," 5–6.

18. Cheri Pierson Yecke, "Pornography Is Anything but a 'Victimless Crime,'" *Core Issues: Pornography* (December 8, 2004), www.cwfa.org/articledisplay.asp?id=6990&department=CWA&categoryid=pornography.

19. Janet LaRue, "Pornography Facts and Figures," *Core Issues: Pornography* (November 19, 2002), www.cwfa.org.

20. Rosaline Bush, "Adoption—the Loving Option," *Family Voice* (January 1997): 16.

21. Linda Lovelace, *Ordeal* (New York: Citadel, 1980).

22. Bush, "Caught in the Web of Porn," 9–10.

23. *United States v. American Library Association*. In June 2003, the U.S. Supreme Court handed down a ruling consistent with CWA's position in the case.

24. Center for the Advancement of Women, *Progress and Perils*.

25. J. Robert Flores, "Blind to the Law," *Family Voice* (November–December 2000): 22.

26. Schwartz interview.

27. Vanessa Warner and Trudy Hutchens, "Kids and Sex: The Kinsey Connection," *Family Voice* (June 1997): 4–17.

28. Sommers, *Who Stole Feminism?*

29. See Rhonda Hammer, *Antifeminism and Family Terrorism* (Lanham, MD: Rowman and Littlefield, 2002), for a repudiation of Sommers's claims.

30. Gerald McOscar, "Slap Your Spouse, Lose Your House," *Women's Quarterly* (Spring 1997): 11–12.

31. Kimberly Schuld, "Stop Beating Me, I've Got to Make a Phone Call," *Women's Quarterly* (Autumn 1999): 21.

32. Sally Satel, "It's Always His Fault," *Women's Quarterly* (Summer 1997): 5.

33. Anita Blair and Charmaine Yoest, "False Factoids, Deceitful Data," *Ex Femina* (January 2000): 19.

34. IWF, "The IWF Weighs in at the Supreme Court," *Making News* (November 1, 2000), www.iwf.org/news.

35. Jennifer Braceras, *Cornerstones of American Democracy: An IWF Special Report* (Washington, DC: Independent Women's Forum, 2002).

36. Brzonkala was the plaintiff in *U.S. v. Morrison*.

37. Anita Blair, "The Fine Print of Domestic Violence Laws," (January 1, 2000), www.iwf.org/media/media.detail.asp?ArticleID=396.

38. Young, *Domestic Violence*, 36.

39. Anita Blair, "Capitol Hill Briefing on Domestic Violence," *Media* (April 1, 2001), http://www.iwf.org/media/media_detail.asp?ArticleID=374.

40. Richard J. Gelles, "The Missing Persons of Domestic Violence: Battered Men," *Women's Quarterly* (Autumn 1999): 18–22.

41. Gerald McOscar, "Teens Behaving Badly," *Women's Quarterly* (Summer 2000): 23.

42. Satel, "It's Always His Fault," 6.

43. Randy Albelda and Ann Withorn, *Lost Ground* (Cambridge, MA: South End, 2002); Dorothy Roberts, *Killing the Black Body* (New York: Pantheon, 1997).

44. Murray-Wellstone Family Violence Option amendment.

45. Sally Satel, "The Abuse Excuse," *Women's Quarterly* (Winter 1998): 17.

46. The national feminist organizations that have devoted considerable resources to this issue include National Women's Law Center, National Organization for Women, and American Association of University Women. Law professor and activist Catharine MacKinnon has also been instrumental in defining "sexual harassment" and pushing for the prosecution of perpetrators.

47. Rhode, *Justice and Gender*, 231.

48. Stolba interview.

49. Stolba is referring to feminist law professor Catharine MacKinnon, whose pioneering efforts led to greater attention to and advocacy for sexual harassment laws.

50. Stolba interview.

51. IWF, "Supreme Court Morrison Ruling Is Right" (May 15, 2000), www.iwf.org/issues.

52. Elizabeth Larson, "Shrinking Violets at the Office," *Women's Quarterly* (Spring 1996): 8.

53. Satel, "It's Always His Fault," 5.

54. Schuld, "Stop Beating Me, I've Got to Make a Phone Call."

55. Hammer, *Antifeminism and Family Terrorism*; Hardisty, *Mobilizing Resentment*.

56. Independent Women's Forum, "Nancy M. Pfotenhauer, Margot Hill Appointed to the VAWA Advisory Committee" (December 3, 2002), www.iwf.org/issues.

57. Faludi, *Backlash*.

Chapter Five

1. I use the term "family" here as CWA and IWF employ it—to refer to heterosexual married couples with children.
2. Diamond, *Roads to Dominion*.
3. Diamond, *Roads to Dominion*.
4. Diamond, *Roads to Dominion*, 171.
5. John C. Green and Nathan S. Bigelow, "The Christian Right Goes to Washington: Social Movement Resources and the Legislative Process," in *The Interest Group Connection*, ed. Paul Herrnson, Ronald Shaiko, and Clyde Wilcox (Washington, DC: Congressional Quarterly Press, 2005), 189–211; McGirr, *Suburban Warriors: The Origins of the New American Right*; James L. Guth, "The Politics of the Christian Right," in *Religion and the Culture Wars: Dispatches from the Front*, ed. John C. Green et al. (Lanham, MD: Rowman and Littlefield, 1996), 7–29; Moen, *The Transformation of the Christian Right*.
6. Annelise Orleck, "Good Motherhood as Patriotism: Mothers on the Right," in *The Politics of Motherhood*, ed. Alexis Jetter, Annelise Orleck, and Diana Taylor (Hanover, NH: University Press of New England, 1997), 225.
7. Burack and Josephson, "Women and the American New Right: Feminist Interventions"; Kintz, *Between Jesus and the Marketplace: The Emotions That Matter in Right-Wing America*; Mansbridge, *Why We Lost the ERA*; Luker, *Abortion and the Politics of Motherhood*; Conover and Gray, *Feminism and the New Right: Conflict over the American Family*.
8. Anonymous IWF board member interview.
9. Franceski interview.
10. Sharon Hays, *The Cultural Contradictions of Motherhood* (New Haven, CT: Yale University Press, 1996), 9.
11. Hays, *The Cultural Contradictions of Motherhood*.
12. LaHaye, *The Desires of a Woman's Heart*, 137.
13. Bush interview.
14. Silberman interview.
15. Dana Mack, "Ozzie and Harriet Redux," *Women's Quarterly* (Spring 1997): 19.
16. Concerned Women for America, "Federal Child Care Emerging Again," *CWA Resource Library* (April 20, 1999), www.cwfa.org.
17. David Eddie, "Daddy Direst," *Women's Quarterly* (Spring 1998): 8–9.
18. Janice Shaw Crouse, "Nothing Can Replace Mom's Care," *Culture and Family* (October 4, 2005), www.cultureandfamily.org.
19. Carrie L. Lukas, "Mothers Don't Go on Strike" (May 12, 2006), www.iwf.org.
20. U.S. Bureau of Labor Statistics, 2006, "Employment Characteristics of Families in 2006," www.bls.gov.
21. Center for the Advancement of Women, *Progress and Perils*.
22. CBS News Poll, "Women: Work, Family and Feminism" (May 14, 2006), www.cbsnews.com/htdocs/pdf/poll_051406_cbs.pdf

23. Pew Research Center, *Motherhood Today: A Tough Job, Less Ably Done* (Washington, DC: Pew Research Center, 1997).

24. Ann Crittenden, *The Price of Motherhood: Why the Most Important Job in the World Is Still the Least Valued* (New York: Owl, 2002); Sonya Michel, *Children's Interests/Mother's Interests: The Shaping of America's Child Care Policy* (New Haven, CT: Yale University Press, 1999); Mary Frances Berry, *The Politics of Parenthood: Childcare, Women's Rights and the Myth of the Good Mother* (New York: Viking, 1993); Emily Stoper, "Alternative Work Patterns and the Double Life," in *Women, Power and Policy*, ed. Ellen Boneparth and Emily Stoper (New York: Pergamon, 1988), 93–112.

25. McBride Stetson, *Women's Rights in the U.S.A.: Policy Debates and Gender Roles*; Conway, Ahern, and Steuernagel, *Women and Public Policy*; Gelb and Palley, *Women and Public Policies*.

26. LaHaye, *The Desires of a Woman's Heart*, 137–38.

27. Danielle Crittenden, "Diary," *Women's Quarterly* (Spring 1998): 26.

28. Mona Charen, "It May Not Be Destiny but…," *Women's Quarterly* (Spring 1998): 22.

29. Pate interview.

30. Betty Friedan, *The Feminine Mystique* (New York: Dell, 1963).

31. Zillah Eisenstein, "Constructing a Theory of Capitalist Patriarchy and Socialist Feminism," in *Women, Class and the Feminist Imagination*, ed. Karen V. Hansen and Ilene J. Philipson (Philadelphia, PA: Temple University Press, 1990), 114–45.

32. Shulamith Firestone, *The Dialectic of Sex: The Case for Feminist Revolution* (New York: Bantam, 1970).

33. Melinda Ledden Sidak, "They Make Such Lovely Pets," *Women's Quarterly* (Spring 1998): 11.

34. Meghan Cox Gurdon, "She's Back," *Women's Quarterly* (Spring 1998): 7.

35. Gurdon, "She's Back," 7.

36. Rosen, *The World Split Open: How the Modern Women's Movement Changed America*.

37. Roth, *Making Women Pay: The Hidden Costs of Fetal Rights*; Cynthia Daniels, *At Women's Expense: State Power and the Politics of Fetal Rights* (Cambridge, MA: Harvard University Press, 1996).

38. Marshall, "Marilyn vs. Hillary: Women's Place in New Right Politics."

39. Bush interview.

40. McGirr, *Suburban Warriors: The Origins of the New American Right*.

41. Carrie L. Lukas, "Women: Divorce the State" (August 8, 2004), www.iwf.org.

42. Darcy Olsen, "What Crisis?" *Women's Quarterly* (Spring 1998): 17.

43. Senator Hutchison worked with Senator Barbara Mikulski (D-MD) to amend the Small Business Job Protection Act of 1996 to allow nonworking spouses of working spouses to contribute $2,000 a year to an Individual Retirement Account (IRA). Previously, nonworking spouses were only allowed to add $250 to these retirement plans.

44. Pate interview.

45. Arlie Hochschild, *The Second Shift: Working Parents and the Revolution at Home* (New York: Viking Penguin, 1989).

46. Diana Furchtgott-Roth and Christine Stolba, *Women's Figures: An Illustrated Guide to the Economic Progress of Women in America* (Washington, DC: AEI, 1999).

47. Green, "The Christian Right and the 1994 Elections."

Chapter Six

1. Boston Women's Health Collective, *Our Bodies, Ourselves* (New York: Touchstone, 2005).

2. CCWI lost staff, funding, and status when congressional caucuses were essentially eliminated in 1995 under the leadership of Representative Newt Gingrich (R-GA). Women members of Congress are still organized as a membership group under the same name, but CCWI lacks the force it once had. In response, the nonprofit Women's Policy Inc. was formed to take on some of the tasks formerly accomplished by CCWI and to monitor legislation affecting women.

3. Patricia Schroeder and Olympia Snowe, "The Politics of Women's Health," in *American Woman: A Status Report*, ed. Cynthia B. Costello and Anne J. Stone (Washington, DC: Women's Research and Education Institute, 1994), 91–108.

4. CWA refers to the intrauterine device (IUD), Norplant, Depo-Provera, and the pill as "abortifacients" on the grounds that each of these forms of birth control affect the uterine lining and could, in theory, prevent a fertilized egg, or embryo, from becoming implanted in a woman's uterus. Since CWA recognizes the term "human embryo" to be the same as "unborn child," intentionally making the uterus unable to retain an embryo is considered equivalent to having an abortion. Proponents of the pill agree that this would be rare, and according to the American College of Obstetricians and Gynecologists (ACOG), the "primary contraceptive effect of all the non-barrier methods...is to prevent ovulation and/or fertilization." It also notes that contraceptive actions for all nonbarrier methods may "affect the process beyond fertilization but prior to pregnancy" (Rachel Benson Gold, "The Implications of Defining When a Woman Is Pregnant," *Guttmacher Report*, May 2005:10). If that occurs, and the uterine lining has been thinned, the fertilized egg cannot be implanted, resulting in what CWA calls a "chemical abortion" (CWA, *High-Tech "Birth Control": Health Care or Health Risk*, 2005, www.cwfa.org/brochures/birth-control.pdf). ACOG's position is meant to define when pregnancy begins, whereas CWA's stance reflects its beliefs about the origins of fetal life.

5. Pew Research Center, "Pragmatic Americans: Liberal and Conservative on Social Issues" (August 3, 2006), http://pewforum.org/publications/surveys/social-issues-06.pdf.

6. Jessica Wadkins, "Reaching Abortion's Second Victims," *Family Voice* (January 1999): 2.

7. Concerned Women for America, *CWA Declares NARAL's Campaign a Fight against Women*, Press Release (Washington, DC: CWA, 2001).

8. www.cwfa.org.

9. Although CWA calls itself "prolife," I use the more descriptive "antiabortion," a term that specifically references its opposition to the medical procedure and one that would be considered accurate by those on both sides of this debate.

10. Catherina Hurlburt, "Whither Women in the Abortion Debate?" (January 23, 2001), www.cwfa.org.

11. Hurlburt, "Whither Women in the Abortion Debate?"

12. Wadkins, "Reaching Abortion's Second Victims," 6–7.

13. Emily Bazelon, "Is There a Post-Abortion Syndrome?" *New York Times Magazine* (January 21, 2007): 41; Cynthia L. Cooper, "Abortion under Attack," *Ms. Magazine* (August–September 2001), http://www.msmagazine.com/aug01/pas.html.

14. Amy Bryant, "Stopping Crisis Pregnancy Centers," www.plannedparenthood.org.

15. Henry Waxman, *False and Misleading Health Information Provided by Federally Funded Pregnancy Resource Centers*. U.S. House of Representatives Committee on Government Reform, Minority Staff. (109th Congress, 2nd session, July 2006).

16. A 2005 poll found that 46% of American women were "very concerned" that they were at risk for getting breast cancer. Another 36% reported being "somewhat concerned." The poll, a Research!America/Gynecological Cancer Foundation survey, was conducted by Charlton Research Company on July 22–27, 2005 (www.kaisernetwork.org).

17. Marian Wallace, "The Hidden Link: Abortion and Breast Cancer," *Family Voice* (January 1997): 11.

18. Joel Brind et al., "Induced Abortion as an Independent Risk Factor for Breast Cancer: A Comprehensive Review and Meta-Analysis," *Journal of Epidemiology and Community Health* 50 (October 1996): 481–96.

19. Wallace, "The Hidden Link: Abortion and Breast Cancer," 10.

20. Planned Parenthood Federation of America, "Anti-Choice Claims about Abortion and Breast Cancer," *Fact Sheets* (2000), www.plannedparenthood.org/library/facts.

21. Breast cancer advocacy groups, like the prominent National Breast Cancer Coalition, do not support policy efforts that suggest such a link exists. See www.natlbcc.org for more details about NBCC's position on abortion and breast cancer.

22. Tanya L. Green, "Bad Day for Pro-Lifers in North Dakota" (April 1, 2002), www.cwfa.org/library/life.

23. New York Times News Service, "Abortion Study Sees No Rise in Cancer Risk," *New York Times* (April 24, 2007): A8.

24. Waxman, "False and Misleading Health Information Provided by Federally Funded Pregnancy Resource Centers."

25. Chris Mooney, *The Republican War on Science* (New York: Basic, 2005).

26. David J. Morrow, "Maker of Norplant Offers a Settlement in Suit over Effects," *New York Times* (August 27, 1999): A1.

27. George F. Brown and Ellen H. Moskowitz, "Moral and Policy Issues in Long-Acting Contraception," *Annual Review of Public Health* 18 (1997): 379–400.

28. Laurel A. MacLeod, "Mexico City Revisited," *Family Voice* (October 1997): 18.

29. MacLeod, "Mexico City Revisited," 20.

30. Roberts, *Killing the Black Body.*

31. Darci Elaine Burrell, "The Norplant Solution: Norplant and the Control of African-American Motherhood," *UCLS Law Journal* 5 (Spring 1995): 401–44; Sarah Samuels and Mark Smith (eds.), *Norplant and Poor Women* (Menlo Park, CA: Kaiser Forums, 1992).

32. Planned Parenthood Federation of America, "Abortions after the First Trimester" (2000), *Fact Sheets,* www.plannedparenthood.org/library/facts.

33. Heather Sternberg Pulkistenis and Elizabeth Bossom, "A Chink in the Pro-Abortion Armor" (July 1, 2002), www.cwfa.org.

34. Pulkistenis and Bossom, "A Chink in the Pro-Abortion Armor."

35. In 2000, in *Stenberg v. Carhart,* the U.S. Supreme Court struck down a Nebraska law that banned so-called partial birth abortions in part because the legislation lacked an exception for women's health. The PBA of 2003 does not include a women's health clause either, but does have an exemption to allow abortions of this nature to be performed to save a woman's life.

36. *Gonzales v. Carhart* (2007).

37. Wright, "Victims of Pornography."

38. Wendy Wright, "Talking Points on the Morning After Pill (MAP)" (August 25, 2006), www.cwfa.org.

39. Concerned Women for America, *High-Tech "Birth Control": Health Care or Health Risk?*

40. Roth, *Making Women Pay: The Hidden Costs of Fetal Rights*; Daniels, *At Women's Expense.*

41. *Wingspread Statement on the Precautionary Principle,* Document Signed by Wingspread Conference on the Precautionary Principle attendees (Racine, WI, 1998).

42. American Enterprise Institute, "Panic Attack: The New Precautionary Culture, the Politics of Fear, and the Risks to Innovation" (February 14, 2006), www.aei.org.

43. Independent Women's Forum, "Nancy M. Pfotenhauer, Margot Hill Appointed to the VAWA Advisory Committee."

44. See www.nwhn.org/about.

45. Dodson, *The Impact of Women in Congress.*

46. Karen M. Kedrowski and Marilyn Stine Sarow, "The Gendering of Cancer Policy: Media Advocacy and Congressional Policy Attention," in *Women Transforming Congress,* ed. Cindy Simon Rosenthal (Norman: University of Oklahoma Press, 2002), 240–59.

47. www.4women.gov.owh.

48. Sally Satel, "Scared Sick? Unfounded Fear and Its Effect on Health and Science Policies," *Ex Femina* (May 1999): 1.

49. Anonymous IWF staff interview.

50. "IWF Agenda for Women, 2003," 12.

51. Independent Women's Forum, "Nancy M. Pfotenhauer, Margot Hill Appointed to the VAWA Advisory Committee."

52. Anonymous IWF staff interview.

53. See linguist George Lakoff's critique of how conservatives use the phrase "tort reform" at www.rockridgeinstitute.org.

54. Marc Arkin, "The Female Condom and Other Bright Ideas," *Women's Quarterly* (Autumn 1997): 30–31.

55. The U.S. House of Representatives passed a version of tort-reform legislation in 2005 (H.R. 420) and is awaiting Senate action on the bill.

56. IWF, "President's Call for Tort Reform in Medical Malpractice Cases Good for Women," *Issues* (March 5, 2003), http://www.iwf.org/issues/issues_detail. asp?ArticleID=439.

57. IWF, "Take Back the Campus," *Campus Corner* (April 17, 2001), www.iwf.org.

58. In response to these charges, the U.S. Office on Research on Women's Health issued "Inclusion of Women in Research" in 2005.

59. Sommers, *Who Stole Feminism?*, 16.

60. Evelyn Fox Keller and Helen E. Longino, *Feminism and Science* (New York: Oxford University Press, 1996); Sandra Harding, *The Science Question in Feminism* (Ithaca, NY: Cornell University Press, 1986).

61. "IWF Agenda for Women, 2003," 12.

62. Candace Crandall, "Correspondence," *Women's Quarterly* (Winter 1998): 26.

63. Martin, *With God on Our Side: The Rise of the Religious Right in America*.

64. Pew Research Center, "Pragmatic Americans: Liberal and Conservative on Social Issues."

65. Roth, *Making Women Pay: The Hidden Costs of Fetal Rights*; Daniels, *At Women's Expense*.

Chapter 7

1. See Beckwith, "Lancashire Women against Pit Closures," for a related argument.

2. McGirr, *Suburban Warriors: The Origins of the New American Right*; Diamond, *Roads to Dominion*.

3. Bernice Johnson Reagon, "Coalition Politics: Turning the Century," in *Home Girls: A Black Feminist Anthology*, ed. Barbara Smith (New York: Kitchen Table, 1983), 359.

4. Faludi, *Backlash*; Dworkin, *Right-Wing Women*.

5. CWA publishes a pamphlet entitled "How To Lobby from Your Home," which can be downloaded from www.cwfa.org/brochures/index.asp.

6. LaHaye, *The Desires of a Woman's Heart*, 87.

7. Temma Kaplan, "Female Consciousness and Collective Action: The Case of Barcelona, 1910–1918," *Signs: Journal of Women in Culture and Society* 7, no. 3 (1982): 545–66.

8. The platform can be found at http://www.un.org/womenwatch/daw/beijing/platform/plat1.htm#statement.

9. "IWF Agenda for Women, 2003," 15.

10. Concerned Women for America, "Feminist Movement on Fast Forward" (1997), www.cwfa.org/library.

11. "IWF Agenda for Women, 2003."

12. Information on CEDAW can be found at www.un.org/womenwatch/daw/cedaw/cedaw.htm.

13. The other countries that have not ratified CEDAW are Iran, Qatar, Nauru, Palau, Tonga, Somalia, and Sudan.

14. P. George Tryfiates, "Ashcroft Prevails as Attorney General" (February 2, 2001), www.cwfa.org.

15. Angela Dillard, *Guess Who's Coming to Dinner, Now?* (New York: New York University Press, 2001).

16. Center for Equal Opportunity, "About CEO" (2006), www.ceousa.org.

17. Butler, "Contingent Foundations: Feminism and the Question of 'Postmodernism.'"

18. Phelan, "(Be)Coming Out," 773.

19. Marshall, "Confrontation and Co-Optation in Antifeminist Organizations."

20. Marshall, "Confrontation and Co-Optation in Antifeminist Organizations," studied the rhetoric of CWA and Eagle Forum.

21. Carroll, "Representing Women: Congresswomen's Perceptions of Their Representational Roles"; Swers, *The Difference Women Make*; Dodson et al., *Voices, Views, Votes*; Thomas, *How Women Legislate*; Dodson and Carroll, *Reshaping the Agenda*; Richard F. Fenno, Jr., *Home Style* (Boston: Little, Brown, 1978).

22. E. E. Schattschneider, *Semisovereign People: A Realist's View of Democracy in America* (New York: Harcourt Brace, 1975).

23. Carroll, "Representing Women: Congresswomen's Perceptions of Their Representational Roles."

24. Schlozman and Tierney, *Organized Interests and American Democracy*, 150.

BIBLIOGRAPHY

Albelda, Randy, and Ann Withorn. 2002. *Lost Ground*. Cambridge, MA: South End.

American Enterprise Institute. 2006. "Panic Attack: The New Precautionary Culture, the Politics of Fear, and the Risks to Innovation." February 14. *Events*. Available at: http://www.aei.org/events/filter.all,eventID.1246/event_detail.asp (accessed June 13, 2006).

Arkin, Marc. 1997. "The Female Condom and Other Bright Ideas." *Women's Quarterly* (Autumn): 30–32.

Banaszak, Lee Ann (ed.). 2006. *The U.S. Women's Movement in Global Perspective*. Lanham, MD: Rowan and Littlefield.

Barakso, Maryann. 2004. *Governing NOW: Grassroots Activism in the National Organization for Women*. Ithaca, NY: Cornell University Press.

Barakso, Maryann, and Brian F. Schaffner. 2006. "Winning Coverage: News Media Portrayals of the Women's Movement, 1969–2004." *Harvard International Journal of Press/Politics* 11, no. 4:22–44.

Bashevkin, Sylvia. 1998. *Women on the Defensive: Living through Conservative Times*. Chicago, IL: University of Chicago Press.

Bazelon, Emily. 2007. "Is There a Post-Abortion Syndrome?" *New York Times Magazine* (January 21): 41.

Beckwith, Karen. 1996. "Lancashire Women against Pit Closures: Women's Standing in a Men's Movement." *Signs* 21, no. 4 (Summer): 1034–63.

Benowitz, June Melby. 2002. *Days of Discontent: American Women and Right-Wing Politics*. DeKalb: Northern Illinois University Press.

Berry, Mary Frances. 1993. *The Politics of Parenthood: Childcare, Women's Rights and the Myth of the Good Mother*. New York: Viking.

Blair, Anita. 2000. "The Fine Print of Domestic Violence Laws." January 1. Available at: www.iwf.org/media/media_detail.asp?ArticleID=396 (accessed March 5, 2002).

———. 2001. "Capitol Hill Briefing on Domestic Violence." April 1. *Media*. Available at: http://www.iwf.org/media/media_detail.asp?ArticleID=374 (accessed August 29, 2004).

Blair, Anita, and Charmaine Yoest. 2000. "False Factoids, Deceitful Data: The Lasting Legacy of the Violence against Women Act." *Ex Femina* (January):1, 18–19.

Blee, Kathleen. 1991. *Women of the Klan: Racism and Gender in the 1920's*. Berkeley: University of California Press.

———. 1997. "Mothers in Race-Hate Movements." In *The Politics of Motherhood*, edited by Alexis Jetter, Annelise Orleck, and Diana Taylor, 247–56. Hanover, NH: University Press of New England.

———. 2002. *Inside Organized Racism: Women and Men in the Hate Movement*. Berkeley: University of California Press.

Boneparth, Ellen, and Emily Stoper (eds.). 1988. *Women, Power and Policy: Toward the Year 2000*. New York: Pergamon.

Bookman, Ann, and Sandra Morgen. 1988. *Women and the Politics of Empowerment*. Philadelphia, PA: Temple University Press.

Boston Women's Health Collective. 2005. *Our Bodies, Ourselves*. New York: Touch-stone.

Braceras, Jennifer. 2002. *Cornerstones of American Democracy: An IWF Special Report*. Washington, DC: Independent Women's Forum.

Brady, David W., and Kent L. Tedin. 1976. "Ladies in Pink: Religion and Political Ide-ology in the Anti-ERA Movement." *Social Science Quarterly* 56 (March): 564–75.

Brind, Joel, Vernon M. Chinchilli, Walter B. Severs, and Joan Summy-Long. 1996. "Induced Abortion as an Independent Risk Factor for Breast Cancer: A Compre-hensive Review and Meta-Analysis." *Journal of Epidemiology and Community Health* 50 (October): 481–96.

Brown, George F., and Ellen H. Moskowitz. 1997. "Moral and Policy Issues in Long-Acting Contraception." *Annual Review of Public Health* 18:379–400.

Brownmiller, Susan. 1999. *In Our Time: A Memoir of a Revolution*. New York: Dial.

Burack, Cynthia, and Jyl J. Josephson. 2002. "Women and the American New Right: Feminist Interventions." *Women and Politics* 24, no. 2:69–90.

Burrell, Darci Elaine. 1995. "The Norplant Solution: Norplant and the Control of African-American Motherhood." *UCLS Law Journal* 5 (Spring): 401–44.

Bush, Rosaline. 1997. "Adoption—the Loving Option." *Family Voice* (January): 14–16.

———. 1997. "Caught in the Web of Porn: From Victims to Victors." *Family Voice* (May): 4–18.

Butler, Judith. 1992. "Contingent Foundations: Feminism and the Question of 'Post-modernism.'" In *Feminists Theorize the Political*, edited by Judith Butler and Joan Scott, 3–21. New York: Routledge.

Carroll, Susan. 2002. "Representing Women: Congresswomen's Perceptions of Their Representational Roles." In *Women Transforming Congress*, edited by Cindy Simon Rosenthal, 50–68. Norman: University of Oklahoma Press.

CBS News Poll. 2006. "Women: Work, Family and Feminism." May 14. Available at: www.cbsnews.com/htdocs/pdf/poll_051406_cbs.pdf.

Center for the Advancement of Women. 1999. "The Impact of Religious Organi-zations on Gender Equality: A Report of Findings from a National Survey of Women." Available at: www.advancewomen.org.

———. 2003. *Progress and Perils: New Agenda for Women.* Available at: www.advancewomen .org.

Center for Equal Opportunity. 2006. "About CEO." Available at: www.ceousa.org.

Chapin, Bernard. 2007. "Post Super Bowl Feminism: An Interview with Christina Hoff Sommers." February 2. *American Spectator Online.* Available at: www.aei.org (accessed March 23, 2007).

Charen, Mona. 1998. "It May Not Be Destiny but…" *Women's Quarterly* (Spring): 22–23.

Cigler, Allan J., and Burdett A. Loomis (eds.). 1998. *Interest Group Politics, 5th edition.* Washington, DC: Congressional Quarterly Press.

Cohen, Cathy, Kathleen Jones, and Joan Tronto. 1997. *Women Transforming Politics: An Alternative Reader.* New York: New York University Press.

Collins, Patricia Hill. 1990. *Black Feminist Thought: Knowledge, Consciousness and the Politics of Empowerment.* New York: Routledge.

Concerned Women for America. 1995. *Welcome to Concerned Women for America.* Membership Packet. Washington, DC: Concerned Women for America.

———. 1997. "Feminist Movement on Fast Forward." *CWA Library.* Available at: www.cwfa.org (accessed October 2, 2007).

———. 1997. "Hefner: A Kinsey Disciple." *Family Voice* (June): 14.

———. 1999. "Federal Child Care Emerging Again." April 20. *CWA Resource Library* Available at: www.cwfa.org (accessed April 28, 1999).

———. 2001. *CWA Declares NARAL's Campaign a Fight against Women.* Press Release. Washington, DC.

———. 2005. *High-Tech "Birth Control": Health Care or Health Risk.* Available at www .cwfa.org/brochures/birth-control.pdf.

Conover, Pamela. 1988. "Feminists and the Gender Gap." *Journal of Politics* 50, no. 4 (November): 985–1009.

Conover, Pamela Johnston, and Virginia Gray. 1983. *Feminism and the New Right: Conflict over the American Family.* New York: Praeger.

Conway, M. Margaret, David W. Ahern, and Gertrude A. Steuernagel. 2004. *Women and Public Policy.* Washington, DC: Congressional Quarterly Press.

Cooper, Cynthia L. 2001. "Abortion under Attack." August–September. *Ms. Magazine.* Available at: http://www.msmagazine.com/aug01/pas.html (accessed June 1, 2006).

Costain, Anne N. 1988. "Representing Women: The Transition from Social Movement to Interest Group." In *Women, Power and Policy: Toward the Year 2000,* edited by Ellen Boneparth and Emily Stoper, 26–47. New York: Pergamon.

Costain, Anne N., and W. Douglas Costain. 1987. "Strategy and Tactics of the Women's Movement in the United States: The Role of Political Parties." In *The Women's Movement of the United States and Western Europe,* edited by Mary Fainsod Katzenstein and Carol McClurg Mueller, 196–214. Philadelphia, PA: Temple University Press.

Coulter, Ann. 2003. *Slander: Liberal Lies about the American Right.* New York: Three Rivers.

———. 2004. *How to Talk to a Liberal (If You Must)*. New York: Crown Forum.

———. 2006. *Godless: The Church of Liberalism*. New York: Crown Forum.

Crandall, Candace. 1998. "Correspondence." *Women's Quarterly* (Winter): 26.

Crawford, Alan. 1980. *Thunder on the Right: The "New Right" and the Politics of Resentment*. New York: Pantheon.

Crittenden, Ann. 2002. *The Price of Motherhood: Why the Most Important Job in the World Is Still the Least Valued*. New York: Owl.

Crittenden, Danielle. 1998. "Diary." *Women's Quarterly* (Spring): 26.

Crouse, Janice Shaw. 2005. "Nothing Can Replace Mom's Care." October 4. *Culture and Family*. Available at: www.cultureandfamily.org/articledisplay.asp?id=9107& department=BLI&categoryid (accessed December 12, 2005).

Daniels, Cynthia. 1996. *At Women's Expense: State Power and the Politics of Fetal Rights*. Cambridge, MA: Harvard University Press.

Diamond, Sara. 1995. *Roads to Dominion: Right-Wing Movements and Political Power in the United States*. New York: Guilford.

Dillard, Angela. 2001. *Guess Who's Coming to Dinner, Now?* New York: New York University Press.

Dodge, Mrs. Arthur. 1914. "Woman Suffrage Opposed to Woman's Rights." *American Academy of Political and Social Science* 56:99–104.

Dodson, Debra. 2006. *The Impact of Women in Congress*. Oxford: Oxford University Press.

Dodson, Debra, and Susan Carroll. 1991. *Reshaping the Agenda: Women in State Legislatures*. New Brunswick, NJ: Center for the American Woman and Politics.

Dodson, Debra, Susan Carroll, Ruth Mandel, Katherine Kleeman, Ronnee Schreiber, and Debra Liebowitz. 1995. *Voices, Views, Votes: The Impact of Women in the 103rd Congress*. New Brunswick, NJ: Center for the American Woman and Politics.

Dolan, Kathleen. 2006. "Women Candidates: What We Know, What We Need to Know." Paper presented at the Annual Meeting of the Midwest Political Science Association, Chicago, IL.

Duggan, Lisa, and Nan Hunter. 1995. *Sex Wars*. New York: Routledge.

Dworkin, Andrea. 1983. *Right-Wing Women*. New York: Perigee.

Echols, Alice. 1989. *Daring to Be Bad: Radical Feminism in America 1967–1975*. Minneapolis: University of Minnesota Press.

Eddie, David. 1998. "Daddy Direst." *Women's Quarterly* (Spring): 8–9.

Edwards, Lee. 1999. *The Conservative Revolution*. New York: Free Press.

Eisenstein, Zillah. 1990. "Constructing a Theory of Capitalist Patriarchy and Socialist Feminism." In *Women, Class and the Feminist Imagination*, edited by Karen V. Hansen and Ilene J. Philipson, 114–45. Philadelphia, PA: Temple University Press.

Faludi, Susan. 1991. *Backlash: The Undeclared War against Women*. New York: Crown.

Felsenthal, Carol. 1981. *Phyllis Schlafly: The Sweetheart of the Silent Majority*. Chicago, IL: Regnery Gateway.

Fenno, Richard F., Jr. 1978. *Home Style*. Boston: Little, Brown.

Ferree, Myra Marx, and Patricia Yancey Martin (eds.). 1995. *Feminist Organizations: Harvest of the New Women's Movement*. Philadelphia, PA: Temple University Press.

Ferree, Myra Marx, and Carol McClurg Mueller. 2004. "Feminism and the Women's Movement: A Global Perspective." In *The Blackwell Companion to Social Movements*, edited by David A. Snow, Sarah A. Soule, and Hanspeter Kriesi, 576–607. Malden, MA: Blackwell.

Firestone, Shulamith. 1970. *The Dialectic of Sex: The Case for Feminist Revolution*. New York: Bantam.

Flanders, Laura. 1996. "Conservative Women Are Right for Media Mainstream." *Extra!* (March–April): 1–3.

Flores, J. Robert. 2000. "Blind to the Law." *Family Voice* (November–December): 21–25.

Fox-Genovese, Elizabeth. 1995. *Feminism Is Not the Story of My Life: How Today's Feminist Elite Has Lost Touch with the Real Concerns of Women*. New York: Talese/Doubleday.

Freeman, Jo. 1976. *The Politics of Women's Liberation*. New York: McKay.

Fried, Marlene Gerber. 1990. *Abortion to Reproductive Freedom: Transforming a Movement*. Boston: South End.

Friedan, Betty. 1963. *The Feminine Mystique*. New York: Dell.

Furchtgott-Roth, Diana, and Christine Stolba. 1999. *Women's Figures: An Illustrated Guide to the Economic Progress of Women in America*. Washington, DC: AEI.

Fuss, Diana. 1989. *Essentially Speaking*. New York: Routledge.

Gardiner, Steven. 1998. "Concerned Women for America—A Case Study." *Fight the Right Action Kit*. Available at: www.sexuality.org/1/activism/ftr.html (accessed March 3, 1998).

Gelb, Joyce, and Marian Lief Palley. 1987. *Women and Public Policies*. Princeton, NJ: Princeton University Press.

Gelles, Richard J. 1999. "The Missing Persons of Domestic Violence: Battered Men." *Women's Quarterly* (Autumn): 18–22.

Ginsburg, Faye. 1989. *Contested Lives: The Abortion Debate in an American Community*. Berkeley: University of California Press.

Gold, Rachel Benson. 2005. "The Implications of Defining When a Woman Is Pregnant," *Guttmacher Report* (May).

Goldberg, Bernard. 2003. *Arrogance: Rescuing America from the Media Elite*. New York: Warner.

Greeley, Andrew, and Michael Hout. 2006. *The Truth about Conservative Christians: Who They Are and What They Think*. Chicago, IL: University of Chicago Press.

Green, John C. 1995. "The Christian Right and the 1994 Elections: An Overview." In *God at the Grass Roots*, edited by Mark J. Rozell and Clyde Wilcox, 1–18. Lanham, MD: Rowman and Littlefield.

Green, John C., and Nathan S. Bigelow. 2005 "The Christian Right Goes to Washington: Social Movement Resources and the Legislative Process." In *The Interest Group Connection*, edited by Paul Herrnson, Ronald Shaiko, and Clyde Wilcox, 189–211. Washington, DC: Congressional Quarterly Press.

Green, John C., James L. Guth, Corwin E. Smidt, and Lyman A. Kellstedt (eds.). 1996. *Religion and the Culture Wars: Dispatches from the Front*. Lanham, MD: Rowman and Littlefield.

Green, Tanya L. 2002. "Bad Day for Pro-Lifers in North Dakota." April 1. Available at: http://cwfa.org/library/life/2002-04-01_abc-link.shtml (accessed May 5, 2002).

Gurdon, Meghan Cox. 1998. "She's Back." *Women's Quarterly* (Spring): 5–7.

Gurin, Patricia. 1985. "Women's Gender Consciousness." *Public Opinion Quarterly* 49: 143–63.

Guth, James L. 1996. "The Politics of the Christian Right." In *Religion and the Culture Wars: Dispatches from the Front,* edited by John C. Green, James L. Guth, Corwin E. Smidt, and Lyman A. Kellstedt, 7–29. Lanham, MD: Rowman and Littlefield.

Guth, James L., John C. Green, Lyman A. Kellstedt, and Corwin E. Smidt. 1994. "Onward Christian Soldiers: Religious Activist Groups in American Politics." In *Interest Group Politics* (4th ed.), edited by Allan J. Cigler and Burdett A. Loomis, 55–76. Washington, DC: Congressional Quarterly Press.

Hacker, Nina George. 1997. "Porn on the Internet: Is It Free Speech?" *Family Voice* (March): 4–13.

Hammer, Rhonda. 2002. *Antifeminism and Family Terrorism.* Lanham, MD: Rowman and Littlefield.

Harding, Sandra. 1986. *The Science Question in Feminism.* Ithaca, NY: Cornell University Press.

Hardisty, Jean. 1999. *Mobilizing Resentment: Conservative Resurgence from the John Birch Society to the Promise Keepers.* Boston: Beacon.

Hays, Sharon. 1996. *The Cultural Contradictions of Motherhood.* New Haven, CT: Yale University Press.

Hertzke, Allen D. 1988. *Representing God in Washington.* Knoxville: University of Tennessee Press.

Hildreth, Anne, and Ellen M. Dran. 1994. "Explaining Women's Differences in Abortion Opinion: The Role of Gender Consciousness." *Women and Politics* 14, no. 1: 31–33.

Hochschild, Arlie. 1989. *The Second Shift: Working Parents and the Revolution at Home.* New York: Viking Penguin.

hooks, bell. 1990. *Yearning: Race, Gender and Cultural Politics.* Boston: South End.

Huddy, Leonie. 1997. "Feminists and Feminism in the News." In *Women, Media and Politics,* edited by Pippa Norris, 183–204. New York: Oxford University Press.

Huddy, Leonie, Francis K. Neely, and Marilyn R. LaFay. 2000. "The Polls: Trends: Support for the Women's Movement." *Public Opinion Quarterly* 64: 309–50.

Hurlburt, Catherina. 2001. "Whither Women in the Abortion Debate?" January 23. *Core Issues.* Available at: www.cwfa.org/articledisplay.asp?id=1456&department=CWA&category=life (accessed April 6, 2001).

Independent Women's Forum. 1996. *Who Are We? The Future.* Recruitment Pamphlet. Washington, DC: Independent Women's Forum.

———. 2000. "The IWF Weighs in at the Supreme Court." November 1. *Making News.* Available at: www.iwf.org/news/000111.shtml (accessed May 11, 2001).

———. 2000. "Supreme Court Morrison Ruling Is Right." May 15. *Issues.* Available at: http://www.iwf.org/issues/issues_detail.asp?ArticleID=98 (accessed August 5, 2004).

———. 2001. "Take Back the Campus." April 17. *Campus Corner.* Available at: http://www.iwf.org/campuscorner/news/news_detail.asp?ArticleID=121 (accessed June 30, 2004).

———. 2002. "Nancy M. Pfotenhauer, Margot Hill Appointed to the VAWA Advisory Committee." December 3. Available at: www.iwf.org/issues (accessed May 20, 2007).

———. 2003. "IWF Agenda for Women, 2003." Available at: www.iwf.org (accessed October 3, 2007).

———. 2003. "President's Call for Tort Reform in Medical Malpractice Cases Good for Women." March 5. *Issues.* Available at: http://www.iwf.org/issues/issues_detail.asp?ArticleID=439 (accessed March 5, 2005).

———. 2004. "Hot Topics: Press Release." June 14. *Media.* Available at: http://www.iwf.org/media/media_detail.asp?ArticleID=906 (accessed July 18, 2004).

———. 2005. "IWF Agenda for Women, 2005." Available at: www.iwf.org (accessed October 3, 2007).

Jablonsky, Thomas. 2002. "Female Opposition: The Anti-Suffrage Campaign." In *Votes for Women,* edited by Jean H. Baker, 118–29. New York: Oxford University Press.

Jeansonne, Glen. 1996. *Women of the Far Right: The Mothers' Movement and World War II.* Chicago, IL: University of Chicago Press.

Jetter, Alexis, Annelise Orleck, and Diana Taylor (eds.). 1997. *The Politics of Motherhood: Activist Voices from Left to Right.* Hanover, NH: University Press of New England.

Kaminer, Wendy. 1996. "Will Class Trump Gender?" *American Prospect* (November–December): 44–52.

Kaplan, Temma. 1982. "Female Consciousness and Collective Action: The Case of Barcelona, 1910–1918." *Signs: Journal of Women in Culture and Society* 7, no. 3: 545–66.

Katzenstein, Mary Fainsod, and Carol McClurg Mueller (eds.). 1987. *The Women's Movement of the United States and Western Europe: Consciousness, Political Opportunity and Public Policy.* Philadelphia, PA: Temple University Press.

Kedrowski, Karen M., and Marilyn Stine Sarow. 2002. "The Gendering of Cancer Policy: Media Advocacy and Congressional Policy Attention." In *Women Transforming Congress,* edited by Cindy Simon Rosenthal, 240–59. Norman: University of Oklahoma Press.

Keller, Evelyn Fox, and Helen E. Longino. 1996. *Feminism and Science.* New York: Oxford University Press.

Kintz, Linda. 1997. *Between Jesus and the Marketplace: The Emotions That Matter in Right-Wing America.* Durham, NC: Duke University Press.

Klatch, Rebecca. 1987. *Women of the New Right.* Philadelphia, PA: Temple University Press.

———. 1988. "The Methodological Problems of Studying a Politically Resistant Community." *Studies in Qualitative Sociology* 1: 73–88.

———. 1999. *A Generation Divided: The New Left, the New Right and the 1960's.* Berkeley: University of California Press.

Klein, Ethel. 1984. *Gender Politics: From Consciousness to Mass Politics*. Cambridge, MA: Harvard University Press.

Kurtz, Stanley. 2001. "Feminist against Speech." May 24. Available at: http://www .nationalreview.com/comment/comment-kurtz052401.shtml (accessed August 5, 2004).

Kymlicka, Will. 1995. *Multicultural Citizenship: A Liberal Theory of Minority Rights*. New York: Oxford University Press.

LaHaye, Beverly. 1993. *The Desires of a Woman's Heart*. Wheaton, IL: Tyndale.

LaHaye, Tim, and Beverly LaHaye. 1998. *The Act of Marriage: The Beauty of Sexual Love*. Grand Rapids, MI: Zondervan.

Larson, Elizabeth. 1996. "Shrinking Violets at the Office." *Women's Quarterly* (Spring): 7–9.

LaRue, Janet. 2002. "Pornography Facts and Figures." November 19. *Core Issues: Pornography*. Available at: http://www.cwfa.org/articledisplay.asp?id=2793&department= LEGAL&categoryid=pornography (accessed July 14, 2004).

Lefkowitz, Rochelle, and Ann Withorn. 1986. *For Crying Out Loud*. New York: Pilgrim.

Leo, John. 2001. "Miffing the Myth Makers." *U.S. News and World Report* (June 4): 14.

Lipset, Seymour Martin, and Earl Raab. 1970. *The Politics of Unreason: Right-Wing Extremism in America, 1790–1970*. New York: Harper and Row.

Lovelace, Linda. 1980. *Ordeal*. New York: Citadel.

Lowi, Theodore J. 1979. *The End of Liberalism*. New York: Norton.

Lukas, Carrie L. 2004. "Women: Divorce the State." August 8. *IWF Issues*. Available at: www.iwf.org/issues/issues_detail.asp?ArticleID=651 (accessed July 20, 2006).

———. 2006. "Mothers Don't Go on Strike." May 12. Available at: www.iwf.org (accessed May 20, 2007).

Luker, Kristin. 1984. *Abortion and the Politics of Motherhood*. Berkeley: University of California Press.

Mack, Dana. 1997. "Ozzie and Harriet Redux." *Women's Quarterly* (Spring): 16–20.

MacKinnon, Catharine. 2000. "Only Words." In *Feminism and Pornography*, edited by Drucilla Cornell, 94–120. Oxford: Oxford University Press.

MacKinnon, Catharine, and Andrea Dworkin. 1998. *In Harm's Way*. Cambridge, MA: Harvard University Press.

MacLeod, Laurel A. 1997. "Mexico City Revisited." *Family Voice* (October): 16–20.

Mansbridge, Jane. 1986. *Why We Lost the ERA*. Chicago, IL: University of Chicago Press.

———. 1999. "Should Blacks Represent Blacks and Women Represent Women? A Contingent 'Yes.'" *Journal of Politics* 61, no. 3 (August): 628–57.

Marshall, Susan E. 1985. "Ladies against Women: Mobilization Dilemmas of Antifeminist Women." *Social Problems* 32, no. 4 (April): 348–62.

———. 1995. "Confrontation and Co-Optation in Antifeminist Organizations." In *Feminist Organizations*, edited by Myra Marx Ferree and Patricia Yancey Martin, 323–38. Philadelphia, PA: Temple University Press.

———. 1996. "Marilyn vs. Hillary: Women's Place in New Right Politics." *Women and Politics* 16, no. 1: 55–75.

———. 1997. *Splintered Sisterhood: Gender and Class in the Campaign against Woman Suffrage*. Madison: University of Wisconsin Press.

Martin, Patricia Yancey. 1990. "Rethinking Feminist Organizations." *Gender and Society* 4, no. 2 (June): 182–206.

Martin, William. 1996. *With God on Our Side: The Rise of the Religious Right in America*. New York: Broadway.

McBride Stetson, Dorothy. 2004. *Women's Rights in the U.S.A.: Policy Debates and Gender Roles*. New York: Routledge.

McElroy, Wendy. 1995. *XXX: A Woman's Right to Pornography*. New York: St. Martin's.

McGirr, Lisa. 2001. *Suburban Warriors: The Origins of the New American Right*. Princeton, NJ: Princeton University Press.

McOscar, Gerald. 1997. "Slap Your Spouse, Lose Your House." *Women's Quarterly* (Spring): 11–12.

———. 2000. "Teens Behaving Badly." *Women's Quarterly* (Summer): 23.

Michel, Sonya. 1999. *Children's Interests/Mother's Interests: The Shaping of America's Child Care Policy*. New Haven, CT: Yale University Press.

Miller, Arthur H., Anne Hildreth, and Grace L. Simmons. 1988. "The Mobilization of Gender Group Consciousness." In *The Political Interests of Gender*, edited by Kathleen B. Jones and Anna G. Jonasdottir, 106–34. London: Sage.

Moen, Matthew. 1992. *The Transformation of the Christian Right*. Tuscaloosa: University of Alabama Press.

Mohanty, Chandra Talpade. 1991. "Under Western Eyes: Feminist Scholarship and Colonial Discourses." In *Third World Women and the Politics of Feminism*, edited by Chandra Talpade Mohanty, Ann Russo, and Lourdes Torres, 51–80. Bloomington: Indiana University Press.

Mooney, Chris. 2005. *The Republican War on Science*. New York: Basic.

Morin, Richard, and Claudia Deane. 2001. "Women's Forum Challenges Feminists, Gains Influence." *Washington Post* (May 1): A6.

Morrow, David J. 1999. "Maker of Norplant Offers a Settlement in Suit over Effects." *New York Times* (August 27): A1.

Mueller, Carol M. 1988. *The Politics of the Gender Gap: The Social Construction of Political Influence*. Beverly Hills, CA: Sage.

Mulhauser, Dana. 2001. "National Group Rallies Students Who Question Campus Feminism." *Chronicle of Higher Education* 5 (October): A37.

New York Times News Service. 2007. "Abortion Study Sees No Rise in Cancer Risk." *New York Times* (April 24): A8.

Norrander, Barbara. 1999. "The Evolution of the Gender Gap." *Public Opinion Quarterly* 63, no. 4 (Winter): 566–77.

O'Beirne, Kate. 1998. "The GOP's Answer to Hillary." *Women's Quarterly* (Summer): 11–13.

Olsen, Darcy. 1998. "What Crisis?" *Women's Quarterly* (Spring): 17.

Orleck, Annelise. 1997. "Good Motherhood as Patriotism: Mothers on the Right." In *The Politics of Motherhood*, edited by Alexis Jetter, Annelise Orleck, and Diana Taylor, 225–28. Hanover, NH: University Press of New England.

Pastore, Ann L., and Kathleen Maguire (eds.). 2003. *Sourcebook of Criminal Justice Statistics* Available at: www.albany.edu/sourcebook.

Patai, Daphne, and Noretta Koertge. 1994. *Professing Feminism: Cautionary Tales from the Strange World of Women's Studies*. New York: Basic.

Perlstein, Rick. 2001. *Before the Storm*. New York: Hill and Wang.

Pew Research Center. 1997. *Motherhood Today: A Tough Job, Less Ably Done*. Washington, DC: Pew Research Center.

———. 2006. "Pragmatic Americans: Liberal and Conservative on Social Issues." Available at: http://pewforum.org/publications/surveys/social-issues-06.pdf.

Phelan, Shane. 1993. "(Be)Coming Out: Lesbian Identity and Politics." *Signs: Journal of Women in Culture and Society* 18, no. 4 (Summer): 765–90.

Phillips, Anne. 1995. *The Politics of Presence*. Oxford: Oxford University Press.

Pitkin, Hanna Fenichel. 1967. *The Concept of Representation*. Berkeley: University of California Press.

Planned Parenthood Federation of America. 2000. "Abortions after the First Trimester." *Fact Sheets*. Available at: www.plannedparenthood.org/library/facts (accessed April 27, 2000).

———. 2000. "Anti-Choice Claims about Abortion and Breast Cancer." *Fact Sheets*. Available at: www.plannedparenthood.org/library/facts/fact_cancer_022800.html (accessed April 26, 2000).

Pollitt, Katha. 2001. "Mad Bad Ads." *Nation* (June 7): 4.

Pulkistenis, Heather Sternberg, and Elizabeth Bossom. 2002. "A Chink in the Pro-Abortion Armor." July 1. *Core Issues: Sanctity of Life*. Available at: http://www.cwfa.org/articledisplay.asp?id=3399&department=CWA&categoryid=life (accessed June 2, 2006).

Reagon, Bernice Johnson. 1983. "Coalition Politics: Turning the Century." In *Home Girls: A Black Feminist Anthology*, edited by Barbara Smith, 356–69. New York: Kitchen Table.

Rhode, Deborah. 1989. *Justice and Gender*. Cambridge, MA: Harvard University Press.

Rhodebeck, Laurie A. 1996. "The Structure of Men's and Women's Feminist Orientations." *Gender and Society* 10, no. 4 (August): 386–403.

Roberts, Dorothy. 1997. *Killing the Black Body*. New York: Pantheon.

Roiphe, Katie. 1993. *The Morning After: Sex, Fear and Feminism on Campus*. Boston: Little, Brown.

Rosen, Ruth. 2000. *The World Split Open: How the Modern Women's Movement Changed America*. New York: Viking.

Rosenfeld, Megan. 1995. "Feminist Fatales: This Conservative Women's Group Has Traditionalists Seething." *Washington Post* (November 30): D1.

Roth, Rachel. 2003. *Making Women Pay: The Hidden Costs of Fetal Rights*. Ithaca, NY: Cornell University Press.

Royalle, Candida. 2000. "Porn in the USA." In *Feminism and Pornography*, edited by Drucilla Cornell, 540–50. Oxford: Oxford University Press.

Rozell, Mark J., and Clyde Wilcox (eds.). 1995. *God at the Grass Roots: The Christian Right in the 1994 Elections*. Lanham, MD: Rowman and Littlefield.

Samuels, Sarah, and Mark Smith (eds.). 1992. *Norplant and Poor Women*. Menlo Park, CA: Kaiser Forums.

Satel, Sally. 1997. "It's Always His Fault." *Women's Quarterly* (Summer): 4–10.

———. 1998. "There Is No Women's Health Crisis." *Public Interest* 130 (Winter): 21–33.

———. 1999. "Scared Sick? Unfounded Fear and Its Effect on Health and Science Policies." *Ex Femina* (May): 1.

Schattschneider, E. E. 1960. *The Semi-Sovereign People*. New York: Holt, Rinehart and Winston.

———. 1975. *Semisovereign People: A Realist's View of Democracy in America*. New York: Harcourt Brace.

Schlafly, Phyllis. 1964. *A Choice, Not an Echo*. Alton, IL: Pere Marquette.

Schlozman, Kay Lehman, and John T. Tierney. 1986. *Organized Interests and American Democracy*. New York: Harper and Row.

Schreiber, Ronnee. 2002. "Playing 'Femball': Conservative Women's Organizations and Political Representation in the United States." In *Right-Wing Women: From Conservatives to Extremists around the World*, edited by Paola Bacchetta and Margaret Power, 211–24. New York: Routledge.

———. 2006. "'Will the Real Media Darlings Please Rise?' An Analysis of Print Coverage of Feminist and Conservative Women's Organizations." Paper presented at the Western Political Science Association Meetings, Albuquerque, NM. March.

Schroeder, Patricia, and Olympia Snowe. 1994. "The Politics of Women's Health." In *American Woman: A Status Report*, edited by Cynthia B. Costello and Anne J. Stone, 91–108. Washington, DC: Women's Research and Education Institute.

Schuld, Kimberly. 1999. "Stop Beating Me, I've Got to Make a Phone Call." *Women's Quarterly* (Autumn): 21.

Schwartz, Michael. 2004. "Marriage Wins the Day in Congress." July 23. Available at: www.cwfa.org/articledisplay.asp?id=6019&department=CWA&categoryid=family (accessed February 5, 2008).

Sidak, Melinda Ledden. 1998. "They Make Such Lovely Pets." *Women's Quarterly* (Spring): 11–12.

Snow, David A., and Robert D. Benford. 1988. "Ideology, Frame Resonance, and Participant Mobilization." *International Social Movement Research* 1: 197–217.

Snow, David A., E. Burke Rochford, Jr., Steven K. Worden, and Robert D. Benford. 1986. "Frame Alignment Processes, Micromobilization, and Movement Participation." *American Sociological Review* 51 (August): 464–81.

Sommers, Christina Hoff. 1994. *Who Stole Feminism? How Women Have Betrayed Women*. New York: Touchstone.

Spindel, Barbara. 2003. "Conservatism as the 'Sensible Middle': The Independent Women's Forum, Politics and the Media." *Social Text* 21, no. 4 (Winter): 99–125.

Spivak, Gayatri. 1993. *Outside in the Teaching Machine*. New York: Routledge.

Stevenson, Louise. 1979. "Women Anti-Suffragists in the 1915 Massachusetts Campaign." *New England Quarterly* 52, no. 1 (March): 80–93.

Stone, Deborah. 2002. *Policy Paradox: The Art of Political Decision Making*. New York: Norton.

Stoper, Emily. 1988. "Alternative Work Patterns and the Double Life." In *Women, Power and Policy*, edited by Ellen Boneparth and Emily Stoper, 93–112. New York: Pergamon.

Strolovitch, Dara. 2007. *Affirmative Advocacy: Race, Class and Gender in Interest Group Politics*. Chicago, IL: University of Chicago Press.

Swers, Michelle. 2002. *The Difference Women Make*. Chicago, IL: University of Chicago Press.

Tarrow, Sidney. 1992. "Mentalities, Political Cultures, and Collective Action Frames." In *Frontiers in Social Movement Theory*, edited by Aldon D. Morris and Carol McClurg Mueller, 174–202. New Haven, CT: Yale University Press.

Thomas, Sue. 1994. *How Women Legislate*. New York: Oxford University Press.

Tolleson-Rinehart, Sue. 1992. *Gender Consciousness and Politics*. New York: Routledge.

Truman, David B. 1951. *The Governmental Process: Political Interests and Public Opinion*. New York: Knopf.

Wadkins, Jessica. 1999. "Reaching Abortion's Second Victims." *Family Voice* (January): 4–9.

Wallace, Marian. 1997. "The Hidden Link: Abortion and Breast Cancer." *Family Voice* (January): 10–11.

Warner, Vanessa, and Trudy Hutchens. 1997. "Kids and Sex: The Kinsey Connection." *Family Voice* (June): 4–17.

Waxman, Henry. 2006. *False and Misleading Health Information Provided by Federally Funded Pregnancy Resource Centers* (109th Congress, 2nd sess.). U.S. House of Representatives Committee on Government Reform—Minority Staff.

Wilcox, Clyde. 2007. "Of Movements and Metaphors: The Co-Evolution of the Christian Right and the GOP." Paper presented at the Christian Conservative Movement and American Democracy meeting, Russell Sage Foundation, NY.

Wingspread Statement on the Precautionary Principle. 1998. Document Signed by Wingspread Conference on the Precautionary Principle attendees. Racine, WI. Available at: www.sehn.org/wing.html.

Wright, Wendy. 2002. "RU 486: Killer Pills." September 9. Available at: http://www.cwfa.org/articledisplay.asp?id=1561&department=CWA&categoryid=life (accessed February 5, 2008).

———. 2002. "Victims of Pornography." January 1. *Core Issues: Pornography*. Available at: http://www.cwfa.org/articledisplay.asp?id=2045&department=CWA&categoryid=pornography (accessed April 5, 2004).

———. 2006. "Talking Points on the Morning After Pill (MAP)." August 25. Available at: www.cwfa.org (accessed May 23, 2007).

Wuthnow, Robert. 1983. "Political Rebirth of American Evangelicals." In *The New Christian Right*, edited by Robert C. Liebman and Robert Wuthnow, 168–85. New York: Aldine.

Yecke, Cheri Pierson. 2004. "Pornography Is Anything but a 'Victimless Crime.'" December 8. *Core Issues: Pornography*. Available at: www.cwfa.org/articledisplay.asp?id=6990&department=CWA&categoryid=pornography (accessed June 2, 2006).

Yin, Robert K. 1984. *Case Study Research: Design and Methods*. Beverly Hills, CA: Sage.

Young, Cathy. 2005. *Domestic Violence: An In-Depth Analysis*. Independent Women's Forum Position Paper No. 504. Available at: www.iwf.org/files/50c58ddao9f16c86b2c652aa047944f6.pdf.

Young, Iris Marion. 1994. "Gender as Seriality: Thinking about Women as a Social Collective." *Signs* 19, no. 3 (Spring): 713–38.

INDEX

education as agenda item, 27t, 33, 38
elected officials, female, 51–53, 134n10
emails, 37
"emergency contraception," 105
empowerment of women, 70, 73–74, 121
"encourage a legislator" program
    (CWA), 32
Equal Protection Clause, 67
Equal Rights Amendment (ERA),
    21–22, 47
essentialism
    feminism and, 123
    identity-based activism and, 124
    strategic, 41–42, 47, 48, 53–54
evangelical groups. See Christian Right
Ex Femina, 129

Fair Labor Standards Act, 92
Falwell, Jerry, 28, 30
family
    in CWA agenda, 27t, 33
    feminist destruction of traditional
        family, 88
    in IWF agenda, 27t, 38
    pornography and, 65–66
Family and Medical Leave Act (FMLA),
    86–87
family planning. See abortion; birth
    control
Family Voice, 62, 129
fathers' interests, 85
Feminine Mystique, The (Friedan), 88
feminism
    antifeminists as threat to, 4
    conservative women's identity politics
        as challenge to, 54–55
    definition of, 7–8
    essentialism and, 123
    family planning and, 102–103
    influence and accomplishments of,
        6–7
    medical establishment, critiques of, 105
    mothers' interests and, 78, 80–81, 83,
        86–87

and negative depiction of conservative
    women, 12
pornography and, 56–58
public attitudes toward, 10, 133n25
representational strategies adopted
    from, 125
sexual harassment and, 146n46
See also antifeminism
Feminists for Life, 99
FMLA (Family and Medical Leave Act),
    86–87
Fourteenth Amendment, 67
Fox-Genovese, Elizabeth, 24–25
frame transformation, 9
framing
    antifeminist frames, 9–10, 58, 69
    ideological frames, 10–11, 58,
        118–119
    importance of framing strategies, 117
    women's health frames, 96–97
    women's interests frames, 10, 58,
        73–74
Friedan, Betty, 30, 82, 88
fusionism, 79, 91, 94–95, 121
Fuss, Diana, 54

Gardiner, Steven, 12
"gender feminists," 113
gender gaps, electoral, 13
gender identity and politics
    conservative ideology and, 51–53
    defined, 40
    ideological image and, 118–119
    lessons from CWA and IWF, 123–125
    liberal individualism and, 121
    media access and, 44–47
    organization into groups and, 39–40
    policymaking and, 47–49
    political activism and strategic
        essentialism, 41–42
    representation and reaction to
        feminism, 42–44
    salience of, 126
    strategic dissonance in, 40–41